FAMOUS PEOPLE

of the

PARANORMAL

Psychics, Clairvoyants and Charlatans

Chris Wangler

GHOST HOUSE

Ghost House Books

© 2005 by Ghost House Books
First printed in 2005 10 9 8 7 6 5 4 3 2 1
Printed in Canada

The Publisher: Ghost House Books
Distributed by Lone Pine Publishing

10145 – 81 Avenue	1808 B Street NW, Suite 140
Edmonton, AB T6E 1W9	Auburn, WA 98001
Canada	USA

Websites: www.ghostbooks.net

National Library of Canada Cataloguing in Publication Data

Wangler, Chris, 1974-
  Famous people of the paranormal / Chris Wangler.

  ISBN 13: 978-1-894877-45-9
  ISBN 10: 1-894877-45-4

  1. Ghosts. I. Title.
  BF1461.W34 2005   133.1   C2005-902315-5

Editorial Director: Nancy Foulds
Project Editor: Carol Woo
Illustration Coordinator: Carol Woo
Production Manager: Gene Longson
Cover Design: Gerry Dotto
Layout & Production: Trina Koscielnuk

Cover Image: The Granger Collection, New York

Photo Credits: Every effort has been made to accurately credit sources. Any errors or omissions should be directed to the publisher for changes in future editions. The images in this book are reproduced by the kind permission of the following sources: Fortean Picture Library: p. 131; *Hanussen: ein Berich* by Bruno Frei, 1934, Sebastian Brant-Verlag: p. 37, 42; Istock (pp. 4–5: Paul Cush; p. 12: Matthew Gough; p. 34: Adam Homfray; p. 101: Matjaz Slanic; p. 129: Brandon Alms; p. 175: Greg Nicholas; p. 212: Duncan Walker); James Randi Educational Foundation: p. 111; Jeane Dixon Museum: p. 168; Library of Congress (p. 30: USZ62-125499; p. 85: USZ62-103583; p. 103: USZ62-66388; p. 105: USZ62-14085; p. 107: USZ62-26516; p. 231: USZ62-96052).

We acknowledge the financial support of the Government of Canada through the Book Publishing Industry Development Program (BPIDP) for our publishing activities.

PC: P5

To the children

On the wings of a dream, the individual flies, hoping to escape the thousand and one discouragements of the prosaic everyday.

—Theodore Flournoy

Contents

Acknowledgments

Shane Kennedy, the ebullient president and publisher of Lone Pine, deserves my gratitude for making this project a reality. Ditto Nancy Foulds, who allowed me to switch hats without mussing up my hair, and Carol Woo, who worked tirelessly to track down the images scattered throughout this book, which were seamlessly integrated into the text by graphic designer Trina Koscielnuk.

During the research, skeptic extraordinaire James Randi lent his wisdom, as did Dan Asfar, a *miglior fabbro* in this genre. I also happily acknowledge my influences, both living and dead, such as Colin Wilson, Daniel Cohen, Slater Brown and Milbourne Christopher. It goes without saying that the non-libelous mistakes are entirely mine; the libelous ones I generously attribute to them. To my imaginary girlfriend, Jo-Anne, I blow a warm kiss. I can't count the number of times I spoke to her in search of guidance. Responding in a feminine voice very much like my own, only higher, she soothed me and inspired me to continue.

Finally, I would like to recognize the generosity, humor and limitless tolerance of "Wings" Wangler, my favorite uncle, bar none. Among poor boys from the slums of Buffalo, you're a very close second.

—CW

Introduction

"I can't believe that," said Alice.

"Can't you?" the Queen said in a pitying tone. "Try again. Draw a long breath, and shut your eyes."

Alice laughed. "There's no use trying," she said. "One can't believe in impossible things."

"I dare say you haven't had much practice," said the Queen. "When I was your age, I always did it for half an hour a day. Why, sometimes I've believed as many as six impossible things before breakfast."

—Lewis Carroll, *Through the Looking Glass*

A book like this inevitably represents a compromise. With a seemingly limitless pool of people to draw from, choosing who to include and who to reject was an unwelcome challenge. Still, I make no apologies for notable omissions, such as Nostradamus or Madame Helena Blavatsky. In general, I have tried to include persons with captivating life stories who tapped into a public fascination with the unknown. I also wanted to cover all the paranormal bases, so to speak: among other topics, you will encounter discussions of reincarnation, witchcraft, fortune-telling, miraculous healings and astral traveling in this book. Dowsing, stigmata, out-of-body experiences and their respective practitioners must be left for another book.

Historical persons such as Emanuel Swedenborg, Count Cagliostro and John Dee make up a comparative minority; these men came from a different era, when belief in the occult was heretical and subject to censorship from church and state. Modern interest in the paranormal shares in this sense of taboo, but grows more directly out of the so-called Spiritualist movement, not the alchemical and astrological debates of centuries past.

Kate and Maggie Fox, two sisters from Hydesville, New York, are often named as the founders of Spiritualism. In 1848, the sisters began to communicate, via rapping on the walls, with a spirit they called "Mr. Splitfoot," who claimed to have been murdered and buried in the basement of the Fox household. When a skeleton was discovered in the house, the sisters went under the media microscope. In due course they took their show on the road, staging performances and séances; by 1855 they could count approximately one million followers.

Although Maggie declared herself a fraud in 1888, confessing that she had no real powers, the die was already cast. Hosts of imitators rushed forward to conduct séances with "sitters," performing acts of physical mediumship such as levitation or mental equivalents such as telekinesis, the moving of objects by way of mental command. I have omitted the Fox sisters, Eusapia Palladino and Daniel Dunglas Home, partly because excellent accounts of them are given in Jo-Anne Christensen's book *Victorian Ghost Stories*. In their place, I present two little-knowns, Henry Slade and Charles Foster, and their bizarre, fascinating feats of mediumship.

Many 20th-century paranormal celebrities either copied or improved upon the Spiritualist method. Even those who took a new tack, such as the crime-solving psychic Gerard Croiset or the past-life channeler Joan Grant, either descended into séance-like trances or used the Spiritualists' "spirit controls"—spirits who offer contact with the other side—to pull off their mental gymnastics.

The decline of religious belief in the 20th century helped their cause, as did a new interest in the paranormal following World War II. The relatively new science of parapsychology became the subject of popular speculation, even making way for the academic research into ESP conducted by Dr. J.B. Rhine at the University of North Carolina. This legitimacy, combined with curiosity about outer space aliens, mysteries of the unknown and Eastern philosophy, allowed for the success of Erich von Däniken's *Chariots of the Gods?* and, in our own time, the channeler J.Z. Knight and "tele-medium" James Van Praagh, both celebrities of the New Age movement.

It's impossible to generalize about the myriad personalities presented in this book. Still, some patterns emerge. Many had rough childhoods and were ostracized for being different, yet somehow remained convinced of their gifts. Some became household names and made a killing, while others, like their counterparts in the world of the performing arts, died in total obscurity and poverty.

Of course, not everyone with an interest in the paranormal is "gifted." Some of these celebrities—Charles Fort and Bernard Heuvelmans come to mind—had no paranormal powers whatsoever; they simply opened people's minds to the possibilities of the unexplained. Others, such as the skeptics behind the scenes, cried foul and criticized paranormal celebrities. Although these crusaders were nowhere near as famous as their empowered targets, I have devoted a chapter to them, as well as one to some notable paranormal charlatans with no powers of any kind (remember Miss Cleo?), who were interested only in money or notoriety.

So, you may ask, where do I stand along the paranormal fence? Before I answer this question, I would like to explain several things. Almost without exception, all the people I spoke to during the writing of this book showed some interest in the paranormal, regardless of their reservations. Fascination with the unexplained and the occult is easily as old as humanity, with roots in the religious stirrings of prehistoric humans. Its survival in our own heavily scientific and technological society makes it all the more impressive.

How to explain this interest? Some lay the blame on popular culture. Perhaps more now than ever, we suspend our otherwise sober judgment to believe in fantastic, wildly improbable scenarios presented to us in films such as *The Sixth Sense* or in the TV series *Buffy the Vampire Slayer* or *The X-Files*. But while the popularity of these presentations lend a kind of credence to the paranormal, I think most people can tell the difference between fantasy and reality, even as the line blurs.

As I see it, the people in this book are remarkable not because they reflect cultural trends, but because they convinced people around them of their unusual gifts, either through public spectacle or publications. Some even became very wealthy in the process. Their ability to inspire belief, even loyalty, in our heavily skeptical and sarcastic world, is easily as fascinating as any powers they professed to have.

My own belief in the paranormal can be traced to Immanuel Kant, arguably the greatest philosopher of the modern era. Back in the 18th century, when science as we know it was establishing itself in earnest, Kant argued that it is impossible, given our limited five senses, to know the world as it is. What we perceive is conditioned, even determined, by our minds, rendering us incapable of experiencing what he called the "thing-in-itself"—reality stripped bare of our ways of perceiving it. So, the question becomes: who—or what—sees reality *as it truly is*? God? The green grocer down the street? William Blake? James Van Praagh?

While I'm unwilling to grant the paranormally inclined privileged access to the Real World, or even one beyond it, I'm also reluctant to state that scientists present us with the *only* reality. Like Alice, who was convinced by the Queen of Hearts to think anew about "impossible things," I'm content to suspend judgment until I've heard the stories, perused the evidence. I hope you'll do the same.

1
Legends

Wolf Messing
SURPRISING STALIN

Moscow, 1940. A small man with wiry hair walks into a bank for the first time. He hands a cashier a blank piece of paper from a school notebook. Then he sends a telepathic message to the man: place 100,000 rubles on the counter. Without thinking twice, the teller fetches the money and watches as the man places it in an attaché case and leaves.

So runs a celebrated story about the Polish telepath Wolf Messing, arguably the most famous psychic to work behind the Iron Curtain. What's remarkable about the ruse, apart from the highly unconventional nature of the robbery, is that it was carried out at the behest of Soviet dictator Joseph Stalin.

Messing was a veteran of the world paranormal circuit by the late 1930s. He initially attracted Stalin's attention because he had powerful friends in his homeland of Poland. When Poland fell after the Nazis invaded in 1939, Messing fled to the USSR. In 1940, during one of the mentalist's shows in the small city of Gomel in Byelorussia, two Soviet policemen entered the theater and led the performer off stage, to be questioned by Stalin at an undisclosed location.

Many such meetings ended rather tragically during the Soviet era. But Stalin summoned Messing to meet with him several more times. When he learned of the performer's purported ability to cloud men's minds, the dictator demanded that he rob a bank to prove his abilities.

Unalarmed, and without much choice, Messing did exactly that. He then showed the loot to Stalin's advisors as evidence. When he returned to the bank later to surrender the pilfered rubles, the teller was so shocked that he had a heart attack. Fortunately, it wasn't fatal.

Stalin was impressed and set another unusual task for Messing: to find his way out of a heavily secured government building. The telepath was led into the building, without a pass, while three sets of security guards were ordered to prevent his exit. True to form, Messing managed to escape; once outside, he waved to one of the officials involved in the experiment, who looked down from a top-floor window with astonishment.

Stalin issued one more challenge to Messing, by far the most daunting. He ordered the mentalist to enter his *dacha* (summer cottage) at Kuntsevo, one of the most heavily guarded residences in the world. Accessible only via private roads, the rather humble structure was surrounded by a double-perimeter fence. Intruders would have to contend with 300 KGB special troops and eight 30-millimeter anti-aircraft guns concealed among stands of birch trees.

Several days passed. Then a short, thin man entered the dacha without attracting any notice. Security and house staff (all members of the secret police) regarded the visitor with respect and deference. The man walked slowly through the residence, eventually reaching the doorway to the room where Stalin sat reading. The dictator looked up suddenly, flabbergasted at the holes in his security blanket.

How did Messing pull it off? He explained: "I mentally suggested to the guards and servants, 'I am Beria, I am

Beria,' " referring to Lavrenti Beria, the head of the KGB (and its earlier incarnation, the NKVD) and a constant visitor to Stalin's *dacha*. Predictably enough, Messing bore no resemblance to Beria, a Georgian who wore pince-nez.

• • •

Messing became aware of his powers at an early age. Born Wolf Gregorivich Messing in 1899 near Warsaw, the young Jewish boy was a devout student of the Talmud. When he was only six, a vision of a man in a shimmering, white robe urged him to follow a rabbinical path. Though a keen student, the solitary, mysterious child was later drawn away from his calling. The first evidence of his ability to influence others came at age 11. With no money to speak of, and on his own in the world for the first time, he boarded a train without a ticket, hid under a seat and fell asleep.

Inevitably the conductor arrived at his cabin and demanded a ticket. Messing later reported that he could still hear the man's impatient voice: "Young man, excuse me…" The quick-witted boy handed the man a piece of newsprint, willing him to see the paper as a ticket. The conductor looked at the paper, then punched it as he would a regular ticket; he told Messing that as a legitimate passenger, he should sit in his seat and not hide under it!

By his mid-teens, Messing was performing in front of crowds, using a variety of techniques. He became quite famous, and after a performance in Vienna in 1915, the 16 year old was invited to the home of physicist Albert Einstein. There he met another famous scientist, Sigmund

Freud, who had been a keen student of hypnosis and other parapsychological phenomena before he devised psychoanalysis.

Eager to test the boy, Freud issued a mental command to Messing: "Go to the bathroom cupboard and pick up some tweezers. Return to Einstein, and pull three hairs from his luxuriant mustache." Messing followed the instructions to the letter, although he asked Einstein for permission before extracting the hairs from his mustache.

In 1927 Messing toured India. During his time there, he was amazed to discover that Indian yogis could remain in a cataleptic state (i.e., in suspended animation, almost like hibernation) for weeks at a time. Messing could also become cataleptic, but only for limited stretches.

Messing continued to tour the world, although he preferred to perform in his native Poland. His powers grew to include telepathy, clairvoyance and mind-reading. Once, he was even recruited to locate the lost jewels of a famous count. Messing located them in a teddy bear, of all places.

One of Messing's prophecies got him into hot water. At a performance in Warsaw in 1937, Messing proclaimed to tens of thousands that "Hitler will die if he turns toward the East." Hitler, who was notoriously suspicious of clairvoyants, got wind of Messing's announcement and put a price of 200,000 Deutsch marks on his head.

After the Nazis invaded Poland two years later, Messing tried to flee but was captured and imprisoned. As a Jew, he should have met the same fate as his family members: death in the Warsaw Ghetto, especially in light of his infamous (and later, true) prediction about the *Führer*. Instead, it is said he used his powers of suggestion to escape his captors. He then traveled to the Soviet Union, where he later impressed Joseph Stalin.

After the war, Messing worked for Goskonsert, a branch of the Soviet government that hired dancers, musicians, acrobats and other performers. Although his powers declined with age, Messing remained extremely popular.

Wolf Messing's run as the Soviet Union's most renowned clairvoyant was remarkable for several reasons. Paranormal abilities were uniformly discredited in the Soviet bloc; psychics and telepaths were labeled as "rogues" and persecuted. For Messing to be given free rein to perform across the USSR was unusual; for Stalin, no less, to embrace his talents was all the more unprecedented.

As perhaps the most significant evidence of Messing's powers, Soviet scientists investigated his powers and published the results in an important journal called *Science and Religion*. Dr. Nikolai Semyonov, the vice-president of the Academy of Sciences, wrote in 1966: "It is very important to scientifically study the psychic phenomena of sensitives like Wolf Messing."

Unfortunately no other group investigated Messing before his death in 1972. Like the American psychic Jeane Dixon, he was reluctant to have his remarkable talents put under the microscope. Still, Messing often spoke freely of his gifts, especially in his autobiography, *About Myself* (1965). The psychic always denied that his telepathic powers were paranormal. "I first put myself into a state of relaxation in which I experience a gathering of feeling and strength," he told one interviewer. "Then it's easy to achieve telepathy. I can pick up almost any thought." Messing claimed to see pictures, not words.

What was the nature of Messing's powers? Some skeptics believe that he, like some other so-called telepaths, received messages through "ideomotor movements"— small unconscious muscle movements and changes in breathing that can tip off a careful observer. For instance, if a telepath holds someone's wrist while searching for a hidden object, a slight tightening of the muscles or quickening of the pulse can show a performer where to stop or when to keep looking. Similar ideomotor gestures can be used in dowsing, automatic writing and other "paranormal" phenomena.

Although these doubts are legitimate, because Messing insisted on touching his subjects during performances, they shed little light on the mind-clouding feats he performed for Stalin and others. Unfortunately, we cannot confirm the veracity of any of these today. It's quite possible that accounts of Messing's feats were of his own invention or served as folklore for people living in an unforgiving communist regime. Still, there's no denying Messing's accomplishment. Much like Mikhail Baryshnikov and Yuri Gagarin, he became a household name.

John Dee
THE CON-CON

Con artists often work in pairs. So do pickpockets. In the world of the paranormal, too, the value of a helpful assistant cannot be underestimated. But what if the assistant sets out to dupe his master—and succeeds? That appears to have happened with John Dee and Edward Kelly, two radically different people who managed to earn money and renown as a mystical one-two punch.

Dee was born in 1527 into a noble family of Welsh extraction. Showing promise from an early age, the precocious academic had earned a bachelor's degree from Cambridge by age 17, and by 19 was made an assistant professor of ancient Greek at Trinity College. Like other scholars of the Renaissance, Dee was a voracious reader whose thirst for knowledge was unslakable. One of his biographers wrote that "he delighted so much in his books that he passed regularly 18 hours every day among them. Of the other six, he devoted four to sleep and two to refreshment."

But the English academic environment stifled him. He longed to study in Europe, an environment more tolerant of magic, alchemy and astrology. During the 16th century, when modern science was only in its infancy, these esoteric subjects blended seamlessly with mathematics and astronomy, Dee's academic specialties. The young scholar traveled in Europe from 1547 to 1551, and was offered several postings, including one at the Sorbonne in Paris.

He eventually returned to England, where he quickly earned a master's degree. Through the offices of King Edward VI, the first of several monarchs he would know, he was awarded a pension and a posting as a rector in Worcestershire.

In 1552, Dee met Jerome Cardan, a born visionary who possessed second sight and other occult talents such as prophecy and astrology. Under Cardan's influence, Dee began to wonder if he too could recruit angels to help him in his studies—and if he could raise enough money to support related pastimes, such as alchemy and divining for hidden treasure. Given his unusual interests, money became a recurring problem in Dee's life.

After Queen Mary ascended to the throne in 1553, Dee was called upon to tell her fortune. Soon afterwards, perhaps aware that "Bloody Mary" would die early and her half-sister Elizabeth would take her place, Dee cast Elizabeth's horoscope too. When Mary got word that he had done so, she suspected political maneuvering and promptly had the impudent astrologer arrested and imprisoned in Hampton Court. A treason charge compounded the insult. Dee was partly exonerated and eventually released in 1555, having learned a valuable lesson about the vagaries of royal favor. Around the same time, in a preface to a famous work written by the mathematician Euclid, Dee complained he had been seen as "a companion of the hellhounds, a caller and a conjurer of wicked and damned spirits."

After Elizabeth took the throne in 1558, Dee's reputation at court improved greatly. The queen's first demand was that he predict the best day for her coronation, and he chose January 14, 1559. Dee was also a talented cartographer, and informed her decisions on exploration; the term "British Empire" was his coinage.

But Dee was not a fixture at court, nor did he want to be. A scholar at heart, he preferred to remain at home in Mortlake along the Thames, immersed in his enormous library, which was the best in England outside the universities. He fit the image of the secretive Renaissance scholar, surrounded by thick manuscripts and outfitted in a worn frock. John Aubrey, a 17th-century antiquarian, offered the following description:

> He had a very fair, clean, sanguine complexion, a long beard as white as milk. A very handsome man…He was tall and slender. He wore a gown like an artist's gown, with hanging sleeves and a slit. A mighty good man was he.

Dee's diary records an escalation in mystical preoccupations in the early 1580s, especially in crystal gazing, or "scrying." Taken from the English word "descry," meaning to reveal, scrying involved prolonged concentration on a reflective surface—a mirror, crystal ball or water, typically—followed by a trance-like state in which strange visions appeared. Dee's crystal was a reflective piece of black obsidian called a "shewstone" because it was thought to "shew" or "show" the future. Like Emanuel Swedenborg, Dee believed another, higher level of wisdom existed, and beings from that plane could reveal its secrets to him.

Dee repeatedly tried on his own to enter a trance-like state and make contact with angels and other spirits.

He appears to have had some successes, but upon emerging from the trance he was unable to recall the spirit messages. This inability did not blunt his desire, however, so he sought another scryer to help him.

A knave called Edward Kelly, who had built up a reputation in alchemy and necromancy (the ability to resurrect the dead), visited Dee in 1582 and humbly offered his services. Kelly, whose real surname was Talbot, came from Lancashire and had worked as an apothecary's apprentice. His pseudonym was probably intended to disguise his checkered past—he had been kicked out of Oxford for an unnamed offense and was later convicted for forging coins. His punishment for the latter was to have his ears "cropped," or virtually cut off, leading him to conceal them with a black skullcap. Apparently Dee never learned of his assistant's earlessness, even though the pair worked together for six years, nor was Dee aware of Kelly's reputation as a carnal and deceitful charlatan.

After descending into prayer, Kelly peered deeply into the crystal. After about 15 minutes, he described the figure of a brilliant cherub, seemingly imprisoned inside and unable to speak. Ecstatic, Dee identified the figure as Uriel, the angel of light he knew from his Kabalistic training. Dee immediately hired the remarkable neophyte and invited him to move into his house, over opposition from Dee's wife Jane.

In spite of his clearly duplicitous method, Kelly proved an effective scryer. Along with contacting spirits with names like Madini, Gabriel and Jubanladace, he was able to receive communications in the so-called Enochian language, a mysterious angelic tongue later discussed by

Aleister Crowley. If Kelly was merely a skillful ventrilo-
quist, as some have suspected, it didn't show: Dee, who
would sit in a corner and feverishly transcribe Kelly's messages, was entirely taken by his abilities.

The messages varied in content. Some had advice on
occult topics—how to search for the philosophers' stone,
how to make the elixir of everlasting life and so forth—as
well as secrets of the heavenly hierarchy and other esoteric
wisdom. Prophecies were also offered, although most of
them were inaccurate.

The exact nature of the relationship between Dee and
Kelly remains unclear. Kelly was interested in keeping the
charade up, so he often became frustrated and repeatedly
threatened to quit, complaining of being plagued by evil
demons. Such inner turmoil helped to convince his master of his sizable powers. It's worth noting that Dee himself had none of the charlatan about him; he simply
believed that Kelly was the embodiment of remarkable
gifts he knew only from books. In a pre-scientific environment, in which magic and the occult were highly esoteric
subjects not readily performed for money or even understood by the public, it's not surprising that a man of such
great learning as Dee might never have clued in to Kelly's
chicanery. His desire to vindicate scrying, and in so doing
earn favor and make a living from it, was probably as
great as Kelly's to keep the wool pulled over his eyes.

Word of their collaborations spread across England
and on to the Continent, especially after Dee claimed he
had found the elixir of life among the ruins of Glastonbury
Abbey, the legendary abode of King Arthur and Merlin.
Soon people came to Mortlake to learn alchemical secrets

or simply to have their fortunes told. With the gold he earned, Dee built up his library and financed his costly experiments in alchemy.

In 1583 a Polish man named Albert Laski came to see the pair. Laski, the Count Palatine of Siradz, had visited with Queen Elizabeth, traveled all through England and was deeply interested in Dee. The queen put Laski in the hands of the Earl of Leicester, who brought him to Mortlake. Although Laski played the part of a wealthy aristocrat, his fortune was on the wane and he wanted to learn how to turn base metals into gold so he could restore his wealth. He was also interested to know if he had any claim on the Polish crown. After an initial demonstration, he became convinced that Kelly and Dee could foretell his future.

Kelly contacted Madini and other spirits and foresaw a grand future for the count. Not only would he come to possess the philosophers' stone, which allowed its user to make gold *and* live eternally, he would also become King of Poland and win many battles against the recalcitrant Saracens. His name, they claimed, would be known across Europe and throughout Christendom. Perhaps most remarkable of all, Kelly noted that Laski was actually descended from a powerful Anglo-Norman family. Laski, like Dee before him, appears to have soaked up every word.

In autumn 1583, on Laski's invitation, Dee, Kelly and their spouses set off for the Continent for what became a four-year trip. Their decision could have been politically motivated, since the clergy in England had been crusading against heretical wizards and sorcerers and Dee was probably eager to escape their religious barbs. After several luxurious weeks in the Netherlands and Germany, they arrived at the count's estates in Krakow.

Kelly and Dee started conducting expensive alchemical routines, forcing Laski to borrow large sums of money. The pair repeatedly managed to convince the count that they were on the verge of a breakthrough. It's uncertain whether Kelly was more to blame for this ruse than Dee, but both began to suspect Laski's money was reaching an end, so Kelly's prophecies became increasingly lackluster. In June 1584, Laski expelled his guests, although he provided them with letters of introduction to Emperor Rudolph II in Prague, who had also bankrolled work in alchemy.

Rudolph was impressed with Dee, a prominent scholar with a sizable reputation, but he did not trust Kelly at first. Dee and Kelly stayed for several months, apparently on Laski's tab, but when Rudolph was warned by Rome to show no tolerance for heretical magicians, they were forced to leave.

For the next two years, they traveled across Europe, looking for charity from various counts and barons. One patron was Count Rosenberg, a wealthy nobleman with an expansive estate in Trebona, Bohemia. Kelly's promises to Rosenberg were similar to those he had made to Laski, and it worked for a little while. By this time, Kelly had learned the magical jargon from Dee and understood how to secure the trust of aristocrats. Eventually his fame eclipsed his master's—but not for long.

A rift had set in between Dee and Kelly. The latter was as quarrelsome as ever and was growing tired of scrying to get by. When Kelly made another threat to leave, Dee tried to recruit his own eight-year-old son Arthur to be a scryer. When that failed, he was compelled to keep Kelly for the time being.

Kelly then received a highly unusual message from the spirit Madini: he and Dee should have their wives in common! Kelly had married a local girl after moving into Mortlake, but since then he had seemed more interested in Dee's wife Jane, who was closer to his age than Dee was. Jane had despised the wretched Kelly since their first meeting and was outraged at the proposal, as was Dee. But Kelly's insistence on following the spirit command, along with a secondary message from Uriel, eventually triumphed. Dee's diary entry softens what must have been a bizarre situation:

> On Sunday, the third day of May, Anno 1587, John Dee, Edward Kelly and our two wives, covenanted with God and subscribed the same for indissoluble and inviolable unities, charity and friendship keeping between us four; and all things between us to be common, as God by sundry means willed us to do.

Whether the agreement was ever "consummated" is unclear, although it was probably the last straw in the relationship between Dee and Kelly.

Dee implored Queen Elizabeth to let him return to England. Supported by Rosenberg, he departed from Trebona in 1589 with an enormous baggage train and guard of 20 soldiers. His arrival wrenched him back to earth: his house and his library had been ransacked, and thieves had destroyed many of his books and magical objects. Nearly broke and with a family to support, he approached the queen, who awarded him a small wardenship. Overall it was a disappointing time for Dee, and he eventually quit and retreated to Mortlake.

Queen Elizabeth died in 1603. Her successor, James, was suspicious of magic and astrology, so Dee had no place at his court. Still, Dee had to eat and support his family, so he found himself appealing to the king at every turn and trying to scrape by with fortune-telling. He died in poverty in 1608 at age 81, not having revealed any of the occult mysteries that had occupied him during his life.

Kelly, meanwhile, had returned to Prague and was promptly jailed. He spent several months there before Queen Elizabeth arranged his release with a letter to the emperor. Now alone and without means, Kelly wandered through Germany and central Europe, telling fortunes and professing to possess alchemical secrets. He was eventually caught and imprisoned again, this time on charges of sorcery and heresy. An escape attempt had tragic results. One biographer describes his unceremonious end:

> He twisted his bed-clothes into a rope one stormy night in 1595 and let himself down from the window of his dungeon, situated at the top of a very high tower. Being a corpulent man, the rope gave way, and he was precipitated to the ground. He broke two of his ribs and both his legs and was otherwise so much injured that he expired a few days afterwards.

Today, John Dee is probably best known as the inspiration for the character of Prospero in Shakespeare's *The Tempest*. Dee's famous crystal, which is actually a piece of obsidian recovered from the Aztecs, is kept in the British Museum along with wands, formula books, a spherical crystal globe and other objects. Dee's key contribution to the occult was in spirit communication. Far in advance of the Spiritualists, he and his crooked assistant claimed to make contact with beings on the other side.

Emanuel Swedenborg
THE MYSTIC SCHOLAR

As I was walking among the fires of Hell,
delighted with the enjoyments of Genius;
which to Angels look like torment and insanity,
I collected some of their Proverbs.

—William Blake, *The Marriage of*
Heaven and Hell (1790)

The term "renaissance man" seems appropriate for Emanuel Swedenborg, the 18th-century Swedish scholar and mystic. Before his death in 1772, he became an expert in economics, physics, astronomy, anatomy and other fields, often conducting research many years ahead of his time. He also spoke nine languages, wrote poetry in Latin, could play a number of instruments and even sat in the Swedish House of Nobles. Then, at the height of his career, he gave up everything to pursue a new paranormal vocation.

Swedenborg was born in Stockholm in 1688, the second son of a professor of theology. After graduating from Uppsala University in 1710, he went abroad to study under some of the period's most renowned scientists, including Sir Isaac Newton and Sir Edmund Halley. Upon his return to Sweden, he was appointed assessor of the Royal College of Mines. This position occupied him for the next 30 years, although he also published widely in scientific

Emanuel Swedenborg, scientist, mystic and grandfather of Spiritualism

fields, designed public structures and created plans for a submarine, a flying machine and even a fire engine.

In spite of the aristocratic circles in which he moved, his contemporaries described Swedenborg as a simple man. In his later years he survived on a simple repast of bread, milk and coffee. He liked flowers, children and pretty women; he asked two women to marry him but was rejected both times. A courteous and considerate man who kindly took visitors into his home, he seemed the picture of the humane intellectual until he began to have strange visions.

In April 1774, Swedenborg had a dream in which he heard the sound of a powerful wind, which flung him to the floor. As he began to pray, a hand grabbed his and he looked up. There, standing before him, was Jesus:

> He said that he was the Lord God, the Creator and Redeemer of the world, and that he had chosen me to declare to men the spiritual contents of Scripture; and that he himself would declare to me what I should write on the subject. Then, on the same night, hell and heaven were opened to me with full conviction. I recognized there many acquaintances from every condition in life.

Over the next several months, Swedenborg's dreams and visions recurred, losing none of their lucidity. His contact with dead spirits, some quite famous, often occurred in broad daylight; he was able to render himself into a trance by slowing down his breathing. As testimonies from his housekeepers show, sometimes Swedenborg fell so deeply into subconsciousness that he could remain so for three days. Upon emerging, he would say that he was busy communicating with spirits in the other world. Yet he was also able to remain conscious of his surroundings in his trance-like state.

Abandoning his scientific work and practical pursuits, he began to write works about his revealed theological system, including his most famous, *Heaven and Hell*, in which he described his hierarchy of supernatural planes. Although Swedenborg's spiritual writings were based on communications with spirits from other worlds, who spoke to him through his "inner ear," they showed the same scientific detachment as his earlier works. With this in mind, we may wonder how he could summon the requisite detachment to write the following:

> The inhabitants of the Moon are small, like children of six or seven years; at the same time, they have the strength of men like ourselves. Their voice rolls like thunder, and the sound proceeds from the belly, because the moon is quite a different atmosphere from other planets.

This infamous passage, and another about the residents of Venus, are instances of so-called "remote viewing" or "astral traveling"—seeing distant realities with psychic powers. Because they disagree with what we now know, they are often quoted as evidence of Swedenborg's mental derangement, which was never proved.

Today, Swedenborg is remembered less for his writings than for some celebrated acts of clairvoyance. One took place in 1760 and involved Madame de Marteville, the widow of a Dutch ambassador in Stockholm. Before her husband passed away, he ran up a bill for a silver dinner service at a local silversmith's. Although Mme de Marteville was certain the bill had been paid, she was unable to produce a receipt when the silversmith came calling.

Mme de Marteville approached Swedenborg, aware of his ability to contact spirits on the other side. The mystic promised to communicate with the dead man's spirit. A few days later, Swedenborg informed the woman that he had contacted the spirit of her husband; in time, he would contact her.

That night, the spirit of her deceased husband appeared to Mme de Marteville in a dream, instructing her to look in a specific place in his old desk. When she did, she found the receipt and a valuable diamond hairpin. The next day, before she had the chance to break the good news to Swedenborg, the mystic informed her that her husband had appeared to him last night but broke it off because he was about to appear to her in a dream!

Swedenborg's most remarkable feat took place on July 16, 1759. Some 190 miles south of Stockholm, in Goteborg, Swedenborg was dining at the home of William Castel. Suddenly, at around 6 PM, he became pale and silent. After excusing himself, he wandered out into the garden. When he returned, still a bit flustered, he announced that a fire was raging in Stockholm, not far from his own house. Two hours later, Swedenborg breathed a sigh of relief. "Thank God!" he said. "The fire has extinguished three doors from my house!" A local governor later took down the account of the fire in Swedenborg's words.

On the following Monday, a messenger from the Board of Trade arrived from Stockholm. Swedenborg's pro-nouncements were true. To lend further credence to the event, Immanuel Kant, the most important philosopher of the modern era, subsequently investigated the event in his book *Dreams of a Spirit Seer*. He was unable to refute it.

Inevitably, Swedish religious authorities took exception to Swedenborg's clairvoyance and unorthodox theories. He was also the subject of some ridicule in high society. Swedenborg went abroad and died in England, where his posthumous reputation would be greatest. His work inspired many people during the Romantic era, including William Blake, who saw the battle of reason and imagination acted out in the Swedish seer. A Swedenborgian religion later grew out of his works and enjoyed some popularity during the 19th century, although its adherents never exceeded 5000. The American Helen Keller was probably the most famous member.

More importantly, Swedenborg's writings were a key influence on the early Spiritualists. He was ignorant of mediumship, which only emerged in the 20th century, but he bridged the gap between life and death during his conversations with the spirits. That he codified what he had learned in theological treatises probably meant he couldn't entirely break with tradition, though at heart he was probably a mystic. It's worth noting that contact with the dead was unknown in his time, since spirits were considered a different kind of being. Swedenborg also put forward the idea that the spirit world is a counterpart to our world, ruled by similar laws, and that gifted people can make contact with it. Today, these ideas are commonplace in many paranormal fields.

Ironically, Swedenborg warned people *against* communing with spirits. Convinced it was dangerous, and that many evil spirits passed themselves off as good in the world beyond, he recommended that only those with divine sanction (like himself) try it:

> When spirits begin to speak with a man, he must beware that he believe nothing that they say. For nearly everything they say is fabricated by them, and they lie: for if they are permitted to narrate anything, as what heaven is, and how things in the heavens are to be understood, they would tell so many lies that a man would be astonished…Wherefore men must be aware and not believe them. It is on this account that the state of speaking with spirits on this earth is most perilous.

In other words, "leave it to the professionals."

Swedenborg's books have not aged well. Originally written in Latin, some remain untranslated and with good reason—he once wrote eight volumes on the symbolic interpretation of Genesis and Exodus. His style was sparse and ineloquent, making his expansive tomes challenging slogs, even for those who were influenced by him.

But Swedenborg's conversion, like St. Paul's vision on the road to Damascus, is of perennial interest. Unlike some other paranormal celebrities, who use psychic powers to earn a notoriety they might not otherwise enjoy, Swedenborg was a very successful man who made important scientific discoveries and even sat with the Swedish government. To his credit, he did not seek publicity from his powers, nor did he incorporate them into a profitable act. Given this curious lack of motive, we may never know whether Swedenborg was insane or genuinely inspired, but his acts of clairvoyance will no doubt remain a continuing source of fascination.

Erik Jan Hanussen
HITLER'S WILLING MENTALIST?

April 7, 1933. 15 miles outside Berlin. Mathias Hummel, a humble farm worker, summoned the authorities when he noticed a human foot sticking out of the ground. Rains had washed away some of the topsoil, revealing a decomposed body in a shallow grave. The dead man had been beaten and shot.

Ordinarily such a case would warrant an investigation. But the Nazis had assumed power six months before, and since then police matters had become complicated. Under strict orders from Joseph Goebbels, head of the Ministry of Propaganda, the head investigator closed the case. No autopsy was conducted. No witnesses were interviewed. The dead man was unceremoniously buried in a pine box. On April 9, an unemotional obituary appeared in a Berlin newspaper, concluding with the following words: "An unconfirmed rumor claims the dead body is that of the clairvoyant Hanussen." The official story was that he was killed by persons unknown. He would become one of thousands of unsolved murders under the Nazi regime.

Few could have imagined such an anonymous end for Erik Jan Hanussen, one of the most famous paranormal celebrities in German history and onetime clairvoyant consultant to Adolph Hitler. His story, told definitively in English for the first time in Mel Gordon's book, *Erik Jan Hanussen: Hitler's Jewish Clairvoyant* (2001), is one of the most remarkable in this book.

Herschmann-Chaim Steinschneider was born on June 2, 1889, in Vienna. (It is a curious fact that Hitler was born only two months later in a town not so far away.) Conceived out of wedlock, he was the son of two itinerant Jewish theater personalities. Usually called "Hermann" or "Harry," Herschmann-Chaim left school early to join the circus and became a talented *Jenischmann*—what we'd call a "carny."

Before World War I, he worked in Vienna as a songwriter and tabloid journalist. The young performer was not entirely scrupulous, and he was not above lying or petty theft to make ends meet. During the war, Hanussen was a soldier in the Austro-Hungarian army. He managed to divine water for his scorched company, so he was eventually allowed to entertain the troops—on strict orders. He took the Danish-sounding stage name "Erik Jan Hanussen" so he could perform at a big concert hall in Vienna in secret. The show was a success and the name stuck. For years thereafter, he claimed to be a Danish aristocrat, even though he couldn't speak a word of the language.

After the war, Hanussen approached the Ronacher Circus in Vienna. He suggested that the troubled circus use a fragile blonde in a strongman routine in which she would break out of fake cardboard chains. The ruse was a great success, and led to the exposure of Siegmund Breitbart, the most celebrated strongman of the day and formerly the circus' main competition.

On the side, Hanussen performed his own routines in music halls. These involved hypnotism, mind reading and fortune-telling. Gordon's book includes interesting original documents, by Hanussen and others, describing his *modus operandi.* An extremely observant performer, he was able to read people through small facial tics, jewelry and other giveaways. When expected to locate hidden objects, he used ideomotor movements (muscle reading) or other means. Hanussen's assistants also played important roles. Before performances, he had them surreptitiously collect information, which he later used to surprising effect. A series of subtle signals ensured that no one was the wiser. Ultimately, Hanussen was a mountebank, but he was extremely confident and charming—he could dumbfound skeptics and make devoted wives swoon in equal measure.

Hanussen plied his trade in public too. He built a reputation as a "psychic detective" who helped police locate lost objects and people. Many highly respected citizens, including businessmen and psychologists, endorsed the clairvoyant. Scientific investigations of his ability were inconclusive, and in some cases skeptics succeeded in exposing Hanussen. Yet some of Hanussen's powers seemed too remarkable to be earthly, and he got the opportunity to demonstrate them during his extended trial in the Czech city of Leitmeritz.

The case grew out of a performance at the Hotel Monopol in the resort city of Teplitz-Schönau. The night before the show, Hanussen became convinced something bad was about to happen, but his manager persuaded him to go on.

Part of the show involved having audience members write down dramatic events from their lives, later to be intuited by the clairvoyant. A manufacturer in the audience had had his safe broken into and burgled recently, so he wrote down the incident. As he and the others chatted and wrote, Hanussen's aides circulated silently through the crowd, collecting details so they could be relayed to Hanussen on stage.

But on this night, a Czech prefect was in attendance, and he had not come to be entertained. Having followed Hanussen's fraudulent show across Central Europe, he finally had his opportunity to debunk the clairvoyant. He befriended the manufacturer, then asked him to add some fanciful details to his dramatic account. The man agreed and wrote that his guard had been shot and badly wounded during the burglary, and that a dog was used in a chase that followed. These details were invented, so if Hanussen "sensed" them, it would be definitive evidence that his "mind-reading" was nothing of the sort. Hanussen did exactly that, parroting back the false details.

At midnight Czech police came to his hotel and arrested him on charges of fraud and larceny. Hanussen and his assistants were jailed and released on bail after 19 days. The trial, which took place more than a year later, was a circus from the first day. Because the paranormal was on trial as much as the man, countless journalists and onlookers descended on the small city of 15,000. The charges themselves were ridiculous. The prosecutors, who requested one to five years in prison, claimed that Hanussen had broken the law by taking money from people who failed to understand what they were buying. In other words, he was charged with duping the mentally impaired. Their arguments were no less ridiculous, as they tried in vain to call witnesses who could prove the impossibility of clairvoyancy and other tricks in Hanussen's bag.

Dubbed "the last witchcraft trial in Europe," the trial dragged on, with neither side presenting a persuasive case.

Sensing an opportunity to break the gridlock, Hanussen volunteered to recreate his experiments in the courtroom. The judge agreed, and the next day the atmosphere in the courtroom was electric. With a blindfold on, earplugs in his ears and his hands firmly around a beloved East Indian charm, Hanussen took the stand. He carried off a remarkable sequence of feats involving graphology (handwriting analysis), psychometry (collecting psychic impressions from objects) and clairvoyance. He was even able to find a key hidden outside the courthouse in a flower box. Over loud cheers from the gallery, the judge had no choice but to dismiss all the charges.

The verdict made Hanussen quite famous. He moved to Berlin and became a fixture at the Scala Theater, where he incorporated hypnotism, mind-reading and predictions into a popular act. He also started publishing astrology newspapers with tabloid slants. Soon he was mixing with Berlin's wealthiest—and most gullible—elites. Gorgeous women were always at his side, and Hanussen was slavishly dependent on their affections.

Hanussen made no shortage of enemies along the way, especially among jilted husbands. One of his conquests, the Countess Prawitz, became his assistant after Hanussen predicted she would leave her husband and join him within six months. But the majority of his opponents were rivals in the field. In 1930, interest in the paranormal in Germany had reached new heights, with thousands of astrologers, fortune-tellers, telepaths and religious cults clamoring for the spotlight. To keep ahead of them,

Hanussen was not averse to exposing competitors; imitators and skeptics, in turn, set out to unseat him, envious of his wealth and high public profile.

Given his high position in prewar Berlin, it was inevitable that Hanussen would run across the Nazis. But in 1932, when Hanussen was in his prime, the party was struggling. Their coffers were nearly empty and some disappointing results in the recent *Reichstag* elections led many to believe that National Socialism was on the way out. Street clashes with the equally fanatical communists, who also wanted to wrest control from Chancellor Hindenburg of the Weimar Republic, became increasingly violent. The public became convinced that Hitler was a desperate, high-strung megalomaniac.

Hanussen, in own his inimitable way, poured gasoline on the dying embers. On March 25, 1932, the headline in his magazine *Erik Jan Hanussen's Berliner Rundschau,* read "HANUSSEN IN TRANCE PREDICTS HITLER'S FUTURE." According to the ridiculous story, Hitler would become the chancellor in exactly one year. No one took the preposterous prediction seriously—no one except the aspiring dictator himself, who later summoned the clairvoyant for a private session.

It's important to point out that Hanussen was apolitical, even naïve about politics. He was asked to use his name to promote certain interests, especially during such a volatile period, and his typically noncommittal reply was that a true clairvoyant, whose only talent is in predicting outcomes, must have no biases. If Hanussen dabbled in politics, it was generally to advance his own interests or to generate controversy.

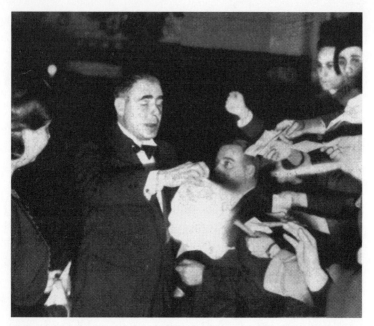

Fans clamor for an autograph from Berlin's most famous Hellseher.

Hanussen's assistant at the time, a Yugoslav-born former soldier named Dzino Ismet, became friendly with
Count Wolf Heinrich von Helldorf, then the Berlin com-
mander of the *Sturmabteilung* or SA, the Nazi party's military arm. The decadent, sadistic count had organized the
first pogrom in Berlin in 1931 and had accrued sizable
gambling debts. Always desperate for money, he met
Hanussen and borrowed from him, which led other Nazi
higher-ups, including Hermann Goering, to do the same.

The Nazis, in turn, provided their favorite *Hellseher*
with 25 SA bodyguards and a private chauffeur. At
Hanussen's request, SA thugs found and beat up Max
Möcke, a rival who had tricked and embarrassed Hanussen

during a performance. Hanussen encouraged his clients to vote Nazi, and in so doing earned the scorn of the communists, who tried to discredit him at every turn. They even released documents that showed Hanussen was anything but Danish.

As a Jew, with many Jews working in his circle, Hanussen must have known that he was playing with fire. It remains one of the great ironies of his life that he was able to make some accurate predictions about future events, which remain inexplicable today, yet he was unable to see that his association with the rabidly anti-Semitic Nazis could only end in tragedy.

Details of the meetings between Hitler and Hanussen remain sketchy, but Mel Gordon suspects their first meeting took place in June or July 1932. The only reliable account of a Hanussen-Hitler session is given by Bella Fromm, a respected political journalist. Recounted in Gordon's book, it was the only such meeting.

Hanussen came to the Hotel Kaiserhof to meet with Hitler. The suspicious Hitler swore the clairvoyant to secrecy, in the event that his forecast was negative. Descending into a trance, Hanussen examined Hitler's hands and forehead and consulted some astrological charts. After a long silence, he said, "I see victory for you...it cannot be stopped!" The future dictator was ecstatic; he had heard little encouraging news of late, and this portent was promising.

Hitler miraculously became leader of Germany (or *Reichskanzler*) on January 30, 1933. Jews in Berlin, including some of Hanussen's staff, packed their bags as the anti-Semitic fervor grew. In one of the costliest mistakes of his life, Hanussen did exactly the reverse: he invited many prominent Nazis to a séance that would seal his fate.

Hanussen's extravagant Palace of the Occult, his elaborate marble shrine to the supernatural, had just been completed. He had spared no expense. Decorated with astrological symbols and sculptures, the structure included a hydraulic lift on which he could be hoisted into the air for all to see, as well as a giant sculpture of himself in a toga, like Julius Caesar. It probably seemed as secure as Hitler's Berlin bunker near the end of the war, and its completion seems to have reassured Hanussen that he was untouchable.

The séance on February 26 was the social event of the season. With many Nazi officials and assorted socialites looking on, Hanussen made an extravagant entry, and invited his guests into his inner sanctum, the "Room of Glass." There, at midnight, with the help of his new medium Maria Paudler, Hitler's clairvoyant made a remarkable prediction. As Hanssen massaged her temples, the slightly drunk actress said she saw red. "Could they be flames?" Hanussen asked. "Yes," she replied, "they could be flames—flames from a great house." Spent, Paudler fainted. Hanussen clarified the message on her behalf: "There are fires. I see a great house being consumed by flames."

Sure enough, the *Reichstag*, Germany's lower parliament, went up in flames the next day.

The Nazis had staged the stunt themselves, hoping to eradicate remaining civil rights during the ensuing chaos, which is what they did. A Dutch communist named Marius van der Lubbe became the patsy, confessing that

Erik Jan Hanussen conducts a séance in his lavish Palace of the Occult.

he had lit the fire to inspire an anti-fascist Marxist revolt. (Some speculated, wildly it seems, that he had been under Hanussen's hypnotic influence.) Sensing the danger, Hindenberg foolishly granted the *Führer* new authority to clamp down on these revolutionary elements; this was basically a license to seize absolute power. The Third Reich was finally a reality.

Still, van der Lubbe's testimony during his trial was confusing. It seemed that such an unimportant bottom feeder, a foreigner no less, could not have ignited the blaze. Hitler was not yet out in the clear, and he was not eager to have stories circulating, via Hanussen or others, which seemed to indicate that outsiders knew in advance of the plot.

Being so well connected, Hanussen surely knew in advance and couldn't resist using it to show evidence of his prophetic powers during the séance. It was a trick he had used countless times in his performances, but now the stakes were much different. The Nazis were paranoid, and Hanussen had outlived his usefulness. Helldorf and others, after all, still owed him a lot of money, and Goebbels knew he was Jewish, so it became imperative to separate him from any association with the Third Reich.

On March 24, 1933, a squadron of SA brownshirts showed up at Hanussen's residence. When they told him he was being arrested, the clairvoyant thought that they were playing some sort of practical joke on him. He realized that they were serious when the commanding officer demanded that Hanussen produce his Nazi IOUs from Helldorf and others. He was taken away, beaten, interrogated and charged with filing a phony certificate to become a member of the party. Upon his release, he found his residence ransacked and the phone line cut. The next day, early in the morning, SA soldiers broke in and dragged Hanussen back to the Gestapo barracks. He was shot three times, and his body was dumped in a field outside Berlin.

Hanussen enjoyed some popularity outside Germany after his death. He was a major figure in magic and clairvoyancy, so American pulp magazines ran accounts of his incredible feats for the rest of the 1930s. As the possibility of war loomed in Europe, some magazines and newspapers speculated on his mysterious association with Adolph Hitler. But by 1942, silence reigned; it seemed that Hanussen had been forgotten.

A revival of interest began after the war. In 1955 a film was made in Germany about him, starring Klaus Kinski; a remake appeared in 1988 starring Klaus Maria Brandauer. Biographies have appeared over the years, mostly in German, as details of Hanussen's remarkable life have emerged. His story, like John Dee's, remains a fascinating testament to the uneasy relationship between the paranormal and politics.

Gerard Croiset
PSYCHIC DETECTIVE

On Easter Sunday 1954, a four-year-old boy named Jacob Klerk went missing from his home in Harleem, a city in northern Holland. Police worked around the clock to find him, using police dogs and alerting all the local police stations. They believed Jacob had been kidnapped, because the only lead was from a local ferryboat captain who reported that he had seen the boy in a passing car. The entire nation waited for news, expecting the worst.

When the case seemed to be going cold, Willem Gorter, commissioner of the Harleem police, telephoned a man with paranormal powers in another city. Gerard Croiset's façade was unusual—he had intense hazel eyes, a bird-like nose and two horns of thick steel wool hair—but Gorter also knew he had been recruited by other police departments in similar cases and with favorable results. That the clairvoyant worked under the guidance of Dr. W.H.C. Tenhaeff, a respected parapsychology professor at the University of Utrecht, made it even easier for him to make the call. After all, a boy's life was at stake.

As soon as Croiset picked up the phone, his mind began to work, even though he wasn't aware of the details of the case. Gorter asked if he would like to speak to the boy's mother. "No," Croiset replied. "I do not want any telepathic influence that might confuse me." Gorter later described their brief conversation:

Croiset definitely stated that the missing child had drowned in the Spaarne River, near a bridge. He said that the child's body would be recovered in about four days. He told me that he saw a caravan beyond the river and a few trailers without a truck. Croiset also received an impression of bales of compressed peat. Two days later, on April 21, he amplified these details with the information that he saw a shipyard with a derrick beyond the river to the right of the bridge.

Nothing turned up in the next four days, even after the river was dragged. But on May 4, two weeks after the boy's disappearance, Jacob Klerk's body was found floating in the Spaarne. His rise to the surface was probably delayed by some object in the riverbed that had snagged him. Gorter, unexpectedly impressed with the clairvoyant's skills, confirmed the details about the bales of peat, the shipyard and the caravan. Professor Tenhaeff later asked Croiset about the significance of the bales of peat. He replied that one of his foster parents used to lock him up in a dark shed with bales of peat and its dust. These powerful memories triggered a reaction that allowed him insight into the similarly charged Jacob Klerk case.

Gerard Croiset's involvement in the case cemented his reputation in the Netherlands as a brilliant "psychic detective." With the help of a prominent parapsychologist, Croiset regularly advised Dutch police on cases of theft, murder and missing persons, and later became internationally renowned for his unusual gifts. As his life story makes clear, Croiset's unhappy childhood was a key element in his investigations, allowing him to fuse his own emotionally charged impressions with those of others.

. . .

Croiset was born in 1909 in Laren, an artists' colony in North Holland. His common-law parents, both Jewish, worked in theater; his father was an actor while his mother worked in wardrobe. Croiset's father, an atheist and socialist, was often away on tour. He eventually deserted Croiset's mother. Gerard, who despised and adored his dad, had no home life and was placed in a foster home at age eight. As he grew up, he lived in six such homes and was chronically unhappy. Sickly and malnourished, he suffered from rickets. He was often punished, and one of his foster fathers even chained his leg to a stake in the ground.

Like Eileen Garrett, Croiset kept imaginary companions and was unable to make friends as he switched from school to school. He later claimed to have telepathic visions from an early age that were a source of embarrassment for him. At age 11, he was returned to his biological mother, who had remarried. The rebellious pre-teen did not get along with his new stepfather. He dropped out of school at 13 to become a farm hand. This career was short-lived, as were subsequent jobs.

When interviewed by Jack Harrison Pollack, the author of the best-selling book *Croiset the Clairvoyant* (1964), Croiset claimed that strong emotional associations from his childhood—with clothing he was forced to wear, being an unwanted child, and objects such as a straw shopping bag—later aided him in finding similar emotional associations with his subjects.

In 1934, Croiset married a woman named Gerda ter Morsche, the daughter of an uneducated carpenter, and they had a son, Hyman, a year later. The jobless Croiset was unable to support his family, so his in-laws lent him money to set up a grocery store. The business went bankrupt in short order, and this failure dogged him for years.

On a summer evening in 1935, Croiset and his wife went to visit Henk de Maar, a watchmaker who lived in nearby Borne. When he casually picked up a meterstick, Croiset's mind flooded with images of de Maar's childhood. When he described them to de Maar, they turned out to be accurate. Croiset had previously been aware of his gifts, but they had never been so clearly affirmed by others.

After the Nazis occupied the Netherlands, Croiset was forced to wear the Star of David around Enschede, the small textile city near the German border where he lived. He was twice sent to concentration camps to work, once because he was suspected of working for the Dutch resistance. While he was released both times for reasons unknown, he become appalled at the inhumanity he saw in the camps. After the war, Croiset claimed his powers allowed him to sense where fellow Jews were hiding and to predict outcomes, such as the death of the son of KLM airlines founder Albert Plesman in an airplane crash.

In December 1945, Croiset attended a seminar on parapsychology led by Professor W.H.C. Tenhaeff of the University of Utrecht, a leading authority on ESP. Afterwards he introduced himself to the scholar and volunteered to have his unusual gifts tested. With his poor education, Croiset did not understand them then and it's likely he never did—at least not from a scientific perspective. The evening marked the beginning of a long and fruitful collaboration.

Tenhaeff ran a battery of tests on his new subject— Rorschach (personality), Murray Thematic Apperception (storytelling), Pfister (color pyramid)—and concluded that Croiset had remarkable precognitive and clairvoyant gifts. Tenhaeff called Croiset a "paragnost," a word he coined in 1932 which consisted of the ancient Greek words *para*, meaning "beyond," and *gnosis*, meaning "knowledge."

Croiset eventually moved to Utrecht to be near the institute where Tenhaeff conducted his research. He did not, however, earn a living from his participation in experiments. He relied a psychic healing clinic he had opened years before, although his energy increasingly focused on using his gifts to help solve crimes.

In spite of what happens on *The X-Files*, police in the United States seldom rely on psychics to help to solve crimes. The procedure is called "psychometry"— gathering psychic impressions from ordinary objects—and it is notoriously unreliable. If, for instance, a psychic detective were to provide inaccurate information, someone could be falsely accused and possibly even convicted. More important, if the case went to trial, evidence from a psychic would be inadmissible since no court would recognize it.

The Netherlands is different. The land of windmills, ING Direct, wooden clogs and Vincent Van Gogh is also an extremely liberal democracy with lax drug laws and tolerance of same-sex marriage. Back in Croiset's day, the Dutch were no less open-minded, so it's no surprise that the local police, on advice from Tenhaeff, recruited the psychometric celebrity in 1949 to help in a missing persons case.

The pair arrived at a courthouse in the town of Hertogenbosch. They were led into the judge-commissary's chambers; there, atop a table, sat two sealed cardboard boxes. Croiset immediately picked up the scent. "Was a shoe found covered in blood?" he asked. "I see a shoe with blood." He was correct; the box on the left held a bloodstained shoe. Croiset continued with his observations, admittedly with some misses. But his images of children found lying together with defects in their necks (from strangulation), and images of them on their bicycles when they disappeared were all highly accurate. He also guessed what their father wore (corduroy trousers) and how many children he had (five others). Most uncannily, Croiset asked, "In what way is Stevens involved?" The suspect's name was Stevenson. As in some of his cases, Croiset's information did not figure directly in the investigation or conviction; the police already had Stevenson in custody. But they now felt confident to consult Croiset in the future.

Croiset went on to work on other homicides, as well as thefts, sex crimes and missing persons cases. His reputation as a psychic detective rests largely on the last group. Croiset was extremely careful not to advise on cases in which his psychic sleuthing could result in a wrongful conviction; that had actually happened once in Germany in the 1920s. It's also important to note that he never testified in court, although police repeatedly summoned him for help in their investigations, especially when all other avenues had been exhausted.

The clairvoyant's specialty was missing children. The Netherlands are criss-crossed by countless dykes, and children go missing and drown there more often than in other countries. (It's no surprise that one of the national fairy tales involves a boy who saved the country by sticking his finger in a dyke.) Because he had nearly drowned once as a child, and also because he had five children of his own, Croiset was willing to help Dutch police in many such cases.

As his fame spread, people from all over the world began to contact Croiset. He helped as many as he could, and almost never charged for his services. His skill was most evident through touching objects of the person in question or by looking at maps, but Croiset was often able to locate missing persons or bodies over the telephone. During these calls, he didn't "fish" for details, as a medium might in a "cold reading"; instead, he let his own sensitivity guide him to the facts, usually beginning with a question, then providing exact details of the pictures that appeared in his mind. He avoided big cities because the sheer mass of emotional and psychic impressions clouded his images.

In spite of his seemingly warm and charitable nature, Croiset's personality was a bit cold. Obsessed by the workings of his own mind, he was incapable of expressing interest in much beside himself. He lacked the patience to hear anyone tell a story, complaining that he could predict the outcome, and was known for his curt, sometimes abrupt manner. These shortcomings are perhaps attributable to his lack of education. A dropout with negligible work experience, he often made simple grammatical mistakes in Dutch or sought in vain for the appropriate word, and his sole cultural pursuit was low-budget western movies.

But those who studied him admired the Dutch paragnost in spite of his flaws. He spoke passionately, gesturing dramatically with his hands, and he managed to seem child-like in spite of advising on cases involving sex crimes against children and murders.

Some cases ended happily. On December 10, 1959, Walter Sandelius, a professor of political science in Lawrence, Kansas, telephoned Tenhaeff to ask if he could consult with Croiset. The parapsychologist agreed, instructing the American to call again the next day to speak with Croiset. When they spoke, with Tenhaeff acting as translator, Sandelius told Croiset that his 23-year-old daughter, Carol, who had been in hospital after a nervous breakdown, had been missing since October 18—exactly a month and a half. After much searching, police were unable to find her, and he and his wife were extremely worried.

"I see your daughter running over a large lawn and then crossing a viaduct," said Croiset, according to Pollack's book. "Now I see her at a place where there are stores, and near them a large body of water with landing stages and many small boats. I see her riding there in a truck and in a big red car."

"Is she still alive?" her father asked anxiously.

"Yes, don't worry," Croiset assured him. "You will hear something definite at the end of six days. But please send me by airmail a photograph of your daughter and some road maps of Kansas and other close-by states."

Six days later, on December 17, Sandelius was about to make an early morning call to Croiset and Tenhaeff when he discovered his daughter sitting in his living room! The details Croiset provided about the viaduct (near the hospital), the red vehicle (she hitched a ride with two soldiers in a big red car) and a dock with small boats (Corpus Christi, Texas) matched the description she provided of her absence.

Needless to say, Croiset wasn't infallible. In one case, he predicted a child's body was in a canal; it later turned up in a crate. In fact, he made many such mistakes in his observations, in many different contexts. To explain his misses, he often claimed that something had interfered with his ability to receive a clear picture in his mind. Tenhaeff almost always agreed.

Others, of course, were not convinced. Croiset's chief Dutch critic was Piet Hein Hoebens, who claimed that Tenhaeff, on whom Pollack relied for the 70 or so cases in his book, had misrepresented or inadequately presented information and thereby misled the author. Given the tone of the book, which warmly embraces Croiset's triumphs and presents only the occasional failure, Hoebens may have had a point. At a time when parapsychology was struggling for legitimacy, Professor Tenhaeff might have had an interest in making Croiset look like a super-paragnost—and could have enjoyed inside access to police information.

Regardless of Croiset's reputation as a psychic detective, his so-called "chair test" remains his most remarkable feat of precognition. Performed some 400 times, it was repeatedly staged by scientists, under controlled conditions, in the Netherlands, Germany, Italy, Switzerland and Austria. Tenhaeff created the test in 1947, modeling it on a similar experiment run by the French parapsychologist Eugène Osty and carried out by a sensitive named Pascal Forthuny.

An unannounced meeting was set up with a seating plan. The seats were not reserved, and Croiset was not told where it was to be held; it often took place at a distance from his home. The overseeing scientist, a disinterested third party or Croiset himself selected a single seat—at random, by lot or freely—and then asked Croiset to describe who would sit there. He was allowed between one hour and 26 days in advance to provide specifics about the person's appearance, career, manner or dress, as well as anecdotes from his or her past—often before the person had even decided to attend the meeting. His predictions were recorded on tape, sealed in an envelope and locked away until the meeting. What made the test so remarkable was that Croiset was often able to see *future* events, as well as past and present.

On January 6, 1957, Croiset was at the Parapsychology Institute with Tenhaeff and some other scientists. A meeting was to be held in 25 days, at the home of woman neither the professor nor the clairvoyant knew. The guest list of 30 had not yet been made up. Croiset selected chair number 9, then provided specifics about the sitter. He said it would be "a middle-aged woman, little woman…she is interested in caring for children." Ten additional details and anecdotes followed. The woman had walked near a circus in the city of Scheveningen; she had been told to go to a psychiatrist for mental problems; and she felt strongly about the opera *Falstaff*. These observations were recorded, then sealed up. Then the invitations were sent out.

When the appointed day arrived, Tenhaeff told the participants how the test worked. He warned them only to sit in the seats assigned to them. Croiset arrived, and his predictions were read aloud. The woman in chair 9 was asked, point by point, whether the clairvoyant's impressions applied to her. "Yes, many of them do," she said.

It's important to note that I have only provided the details that corresponded closely with the woman's testimony. Several impressions were slightly accurate, or even remotely accurate, while several were far off the mark, such as Croiset's idea that the woman had dropped a handkerchief into a cage with a wild animal. For all involved, however, the test was considered a great success.

Sometimes the results of these tests were curious. In one instance, Tenhaeff asked the paragnost to describe who would sit in chair 18 at a meeting in Rotterdam in October 1952.

"I see nothing," Croiset mumbled.

"Are you sure?" said Tenhaeff.

"Absolutely."

Tenhaeff asked him to describe chair 3's sitter instead.

"A woman will sit there. She has scars on her face. I see the scars have something to do with an automobile accident in Italy."

When the meeting commenced some weeks later, the person in chair 3 matched Croiset's description. But that wasn't the coup that night. The person in seat 18 was unable to come, so the seat was empty!

Croiset died on July 20, 1980. Obituaries around the world noted his contributions to various police investigations in the Netherlands and Europe. His critics, however, continued to attack him, and his reputation today is only a shadow of what it once was. Perhaps most importantly, the profile of psychic detectives has not risen significantly in the Netherlands or elsewhere since his death. New methods in police investigation have revolutionized forensics, and police today rely almost exclusively on physical evidence and the testimony of expert witnesses.

In the cases I have included, it's important to note the possibility for cheating. The American professor Sandelius, for instance, did not talk to Croiset directly; he called Tenhaeff first. In theory, Tenhaeff could have called the paragnost and told him about the city and the hospital involved. If Croiset consulted detailed maps, he could have tracked a variety of escape routes from the hospital. It's likely, too, that an unstable person would hitch rides, eventually getting into a red vehicle, and would travel to a city with boats moored nearby. Croiset may have left these details a bit vague, certain that they would correspond with events in a broader narrative of someone's wanderings. Knowing the context could provide him with all he needed to hazard very informed guesses about the events in question.

Take, as another example, the drowning cases Croiset followed. Because it is such a common cause of death in the Netherlands, once Croiset was able to envision typically drowning scenarios, he could add location-specific details to create a narrative about the dead child's final moments. It wouldn't be accurate, but it would *seem* accurate. Similarly, he could guess that middle-aged women would make up the majority of sitters at a chair test or rely on the facts that some of his observations could be applied to the sitters past, present or future—a reasonably large canvas. And even if Croiset made more incorrect than correct observations, he could rely on the correct ones to be remembered.

Still, some of Croiset's predications shun easy explanations. How, for instance, did he know Carol Sandelius would still be alive, especially after more than a month? Similarly, how was he able, on repeated occasions, to name with accuracy the places where corpses and missing persons would be found? We're left with more questions than answers.

Cagliostro
MASONIC COPT OR CON MAN?

He conversed with Jesus Christ in Galilee. He created an elixir that turned a chambermaid into a baby. He was the Wandering Jew of legend, who had traveled the world for 1400 years. He was able, by dint of his skill as an alchemist, to double the size of diamonds and jewels.

According to Iain McCalman, author of *The Last Alchemist* (2003), these are some of the countless rumors that circulated around Count Cagliostro, arguably the most fascinating person of the 18th century. He has been featured or included in dozens of books, some by famous authors like Goethe and Dumas, as well as feature films (*The Affair of the Pearl Necklace*), operas (*The Magic Flute*) and even comic books (*Spawn*). Yet, like Rasputin, Cagliostro remains mysterious, enigmatic. His involvement with freemasonry was a fascinating microcosm of his divided loyalties, also apparent in the society he kept: high-minded, occult idealism, joined to a flair for the dramatic and superficial.

Cagliostro was born Giuseppe Balsamo in 1743 in the Sicilian city of Palermo. Although raised by simple, good-hearted peasants, he was by all accounts an unruly teenager from the slums, and might have led a local gang. He ran away from a seminary on several occasions before being sent to a monastery that specialized in healing. One story tells how the young con artist substituted the names of well-known whores for saints during a prayer recital over dinner. The monks were shocked, and he was eventually thrown out.

Cagliostro probably had his first contact with chemistry at the monastery; the training would aid him later when he dabbled in alchemy and medicine. For the time being, however, he scraped by as a petty criminal, using his gifts for drawing to forge letters, theater tickets, anything he could use to turn a profit. But he was also intellectually precocious, and as his street smarts developed so did his command of the occult. While it's not clear where he learned mystical traditions such as the Kabalah, it added immeasurably to the charismatic air of mystery that surrounded him for most of his life.

When he was 25, he moved to Rome. There he fell in love with a striking 14-year-old girl named Lorenza Seraphina Feliciani, the illiterate but charming daughter of an impoverished copper smelter. The pair hurriedly married, over her father's objections. True to his criminal nature, Giuseppe immediately began to offer his tender wife's favors to aristocrats in exchange for commissions in art or chemistry. Naturally enough, she came to resent this imposition, especially when her suitors were not to her liking, yet she remained with her husband for many years and during countless adventures.

At first they begged their way across Europe, but Cagliostro's resourcefulness, along with Lorenza's endless charms, soon earned them entry into increasingly wealthy circles. Making a noticeable entrance wherever they arrived, they often claimed to be poor pilgrims on a tour of religious shrines and gave alms to the poor. To add to his reputation, the man known as Giuseppe Balsamo changed his handle to Count Allesandro di Cagliostro, colonel of the Thirteenth Brandenburg Regiment and Prince of Trébisond. Lorenza, meanwhile, became Seraphina, Countess Cagliostro.

In 1776 the count was admitted to the Esperance Lodge of Freemasons in London's poor Soho district. Iain McCalman describes the experience as "an initiation in the deepest sense—the transformative moment of his life."

The freemasons were originally made up of stone masons who traveled medieval Europe erecting important buildings. Surfacing in England around 1630, they were a secret society whose basic belief was the benevolence and brotherhood of man. Each member was like a finely crafted brick in a magnificent structure, little understood by the public. With their elaborate systems of secret signs, symbols and rites based on the Biblical allegory of the erection of the Temple of Solomon, the masons attracted all manner of people interested in the occult, although most members were middle- and upper-class males. Their goal was to carry forth a deeply guarded secret, passed down through the generations and knowable only after a long and demanding process of initiation from apprentice to journeyman to master.

The initiation rites, which seemed bizarre to outsiders, varied across Europe. An aspirant might be led blindfolded through a series of passages, wearing a slipper on one foot and a boot on another; or he might hold compasses to his breast, facing robed men pointing swords at him. As a sign of subservience, he might kneel before the master of the lodge, stripped naked.

For Cagliostro's initiation, he was required to swear an oath of absolute secrecy. Then he was hoisted to the ceiling on creaking pulleys and left to dangle for a time; this part of the initiation was intended to underscore his helplessness without the divine. Unfortunately, the rope gave way and he fell to the floor, injuring his hand. He was then given a loaded pistol and ordered to shoot at his head. This action represented, symbolically, the fate that awaited him were he to divulge secrets of the brotherhood. Cagliostro hesitated at first, but upon hearing the catcalls of those in attendance he pulled the trigger. He felt something on the side of his head and momentarily worried that he was dead. Then he saw the trick: the shot had been simulated. He was in.

Cagliostro's personality and talents found a home in the lodge. Here was a secular church with all the pageantry and mystery of the Catholic Church but none of its ecclesiastical stuffiness. When Cagliostro came across a book that traced the ancient Egyptian origins of freemasonry, his mind raced. He decided that contemporary masons had drifted from their origins among the craftsmen who erected the pyramids. As a more compelling, more exotic strain of masonry, this Egyptian variety set its sights very high: to renew and reunify humanity. With its pharaohs, glamor and bizarre mythologies, ancient Egypt was also, incidentally enough, an easy con, highly resistant to exposure by virtue of its mere remoteness.

Cagliostro hit the road again, now calling himself the Grand Masonic Copt. He set up Masonic temples across Europe, and his fame grew. But he was much more than a Masonic high priest. He was a prophet, a summoner of the dead, a healer and an alchemist; a hero to the poor, who opened up clinics and healed the sick for free, and a distraction to the nobility, who showed an unslakable thirst for the sensational, the mystical. One countess said, "Cagliostro was possessed of a demonic power, he enthralled the mind, paralyzed the will."

Cagliostro constantly got into trouble, and relied heavily on his wife's delicate charm to smooth out the corners. Even as he became a very rich man, his arcane preoccupations—sorcery, healing, freemasonry and numerology, to name only a few—became prime targets of the Inquisition, which would eventually unseat him. He made many enemies (often admirers at first), including Casanova and Catherine the Great, and even the most talked-about woman in Europe, Marie Antoinette. Following his mysterious involvement in the so-called Affair of the Diamond Necklace, said to be an important lead-up to the French Revolution, Cagliostro spent time in the Bastille and was banished from France after he was acquitted. During the debacle, he lost all his wealth.

He wandered Europe again—like Aleister Crowley, it was almost second nature to him—but his notoriety preceded him. Upon his return to Rome, a fatal miscalculation, the Catholic church had him arrested; the charges were heresy and practising freemasonry. He was found guilty and sentenced to spend the rest of his life in prison. In 1795, at age 52, he died in poverty and obscurity. His wife, meanwhile, was also called up on charges. Claiming that her husband had prostituted her, she begged for mercy but received none: she too was sent to a Roman prison, where she eventually went mad.

Count Cagilostro looks to the heavens, perhaps the only place he could ply his trade following his tragic decline.

The judgment of posterity was mixed. Most of his biographers granted Cagliostro his eccentricity but refused to believe he had any genuine paranormal gifts. The English historian Thomas Carlyle called him an "arch quack," adding that his life exposed the deep currents of irrationality in the so-called Age of Enlightenment. Even if we admit that he made no lasting contribution to learning or science, and that he was probably more scoundrel than occultist, we still have the record of Cagliostro's life, easily one of the most remarkable of any paranormal celebrity.

2
Unusually Inspired

Erich von Däniken
ANCIENT ASTRONAUTS

"People should learn the meaning of astonishment."
—Erich von Däniken

Paul, a fair weather friend from high school, waltzed over as my girlfriend and I were playing pool at a campus bar. A genius at calculus who became something of legend by pilfering cigarettes from the gas station where he worked, Paul was known for his annoying flights of fancy.

Dismissing with pleasantries, he dropped a big paperback on the pool table, knocking several balls out of place. Before I could jab him with my cue, he declared, "You gotta read this, man. It will *blow your mind.*"

The book was called *The Sirius Mystery* by Robert Temple. In his slightly condescending way, Paul explained that a primitive African tribe named the Dogons had become aware that Sirius, a.k.a. "the Dog Star," was orbited by a white dwarf star. *So what?* I thought to myself. Well, the white dwarf in question, invisible to the naked eye, had only recently been spotted by astronomers, begging the question: how on earth did the Dogons know of its existence nearly 5000 years ago?

Though initially skeptical, I took the book, read about 100 pages, then gave up. Why should I care about these Dogons anyway? In spite of my college education, earned mostly at the bar mentioned above, I could only point out two African nations on a map—Egypt and South Africa.

Now, to appreciate the subtleties of this imposing book, I was expected to become an overnight expert on the Dogon of Mali in former French Sudan and understand precisely how a primitive tribe, circa 3200 BC, made astronomical discoveries with the aid of aliens from outer space?

In retrospect, I understand the allure of *The Sirius Mystery*, *The Celestine Prophecy* and other books like them. It has something to do with what the French call *idées reçues*—traditional wisdom or "received ideas." In our society, many people consider science the dominant paradigm of knowledge. But just as many, especially those with an interest in the paranormal, are convinced that science is incapable of covering all the bases. A major figure in this area is Erich von Däniken, the architect of some unusual theories about ancient mysteries that still enjoy popularity today.

Von Däniken (*Day-nee-kin*) was born in Zofingen, Switzerland, in 1935. Raised in a traditional Catholic setting, he was fascinated at an early age by inconsistencies between accounts of mysterious events in the Bible and official church doctrine. Upon leaving school, he took a variety of jobs in hotels, eventually becoming a manager. The seasonal work allowed him to indulge his passion: traveling to sites around the globe and researching the mysteries of lost civilizations.

The advent of space travel during the 1950s inspired von Däniken. His goal became to link ancient myths, such as the arrival of the Sun god in the epic of *Gilgamesh*, and extraterrestrial contact. In 1961 he began to publish his theories in German periodicals. Eventually he finished a manuscript, based on years of research and travel, entitled *Memories of the Future* (in German, *Erinnerungen an die Zukunft*). A U.S. edition of the book, entitled *Chariots of the Gods?*, appeared in 1970. It became an international sensation, was translated into many languages and was adapted for film and TV.

The book advanced a radical thesis, often called "the ancient astronaut" theory. Focusing on ancient drawings, sites, maps and pictographs, von Däniken postulated that these relics showed the widespread influence of extraterrestrials on human beings. In his introduction he wrote:

> I claim that our forefathers received visits from the universe in the remote past. Even though I do not know who these extraterrestrial intelligences were or from which planet they came, I nevertheless proclaim that these "strangers" annihilated part of mankind existing at the time and produced a new, perhaps the first, *homo sapiens.*

As evidence, von Däniken pointed to cosmic battles in ancient myths and artifacts that revealed the intervention of extraterrestrials.

Take the image of the carving on the next page—one of the cornerstones of von Däniken's argument and indicative of his novel reinterpretations. It is a Mayan sarcophagus lid recovered from Palenque, a celebrated Mexican archeological site. According to James Randi (in a book called *Flim Flam!*), most historians agree that the carving depicts a typical nobleman of the time (center),

According to Erich von Däniken, the design on this Mayan sarcophagus lid shows the outline of an ancient astronaut inside his space capsule.

surrounded by many stylized elements of Mayan art (birds, earth gods, serpents).

To von Däniken, however, it depicts an ancient astronaut, enveloped by oxygen tubes. He sits atop an elaborate rocket—note the mechanical cross-like structure above him—with flames exiting from the bottom. Von Däniken was convinced that such astronauts traveled great distances to earth, made contact with the locals and added immeasurably to their primitive technology. These remarkable beings were later incorporated into cultural artifacts, as gods had been incorporated into the myths and art of other early cultures.

To support his thesis, von Däniken pointed to the mysterious wonders of ancient cultures, such as the Egyptian temples, the large heads on Easter Island and Stonehenge. For years, archeologists struggled to explain how these monuments were constructed, since they seemed too mathematically sophisticated or enormous to be the work of primitive hands. Von Däniken concluded that only otherworldly agents could have engineered such wonders.

To lend credibility to his arguments, von Däniken referred to some remarkable and puzzling ground markings in Peru. In the middle of the desert near the towns of Nazca and Palpa are some giant drawings in the sand, some hundreds of yards wide. They include long, straight lines, triangles, trapezoids and even spiders, lizards and birds. Archeologists have advanced theories about the meanings of the markings, but none has been satisfactory. In keeping with ideas about ancient astronauts, Von Däniken submitted that these markings were a kind of landing site or "space port" for otherworldly spacecraft.

Not convinced? I confess that my presentation of this occasionally bizarre material is not as persuasive as von Däniken's charming, inquisitive style. He invites readers on a remarkable journey of discovery, appealing to our sense of curiosity about the past. Along with enabling his readers to understand complicated swathes of ancient history through a very simplistic contemporary lens, von Däniken's theories seem, rather conveniently, to "solve" many long-unsolved mysteries, all the while generating media attention with bold new reinterpretations of accepted truths.

Of course, when the rubber hits the road, von Däniken's theories collapse like a house of cards. Using simplistic arguments and showing a basic ignorance about ancient motifs in art, von Däniken generally proceeded from conclusion (ancient astronauts) to hypothesis (lingering ancient mysteries).

Worse, very few if any of von Däniken's ideas were original. Myths about advanced beings or gods descending from the sky are as old as humanity. With the dawn of the atomic age, UFO sightings multiplied, and pulp fiction and film creators speculated that we weren't alone. Von Däniken took a growing interest in these popular preoccupations, mostly with no basis in fact, and created a theory based on real events and landmarks.

The implications were unsettling. After all, his research supported a wholesale rewrite of human history by placing the fates of early civilizations in the hands of extraterrestrials. Ancient peoples seemed like helpless victims in an extraterrestrial mission to interfere in earth's history. Worried by this notion, many scientists and archeologists assailed the book. One skeptic, Clifford Wilson, published *Crash Go the Space Gods* (1973), followed by Ronald Story's *The Space Gods Revealed* (1976), an unforgiving, virtually page-by-page assault on *Chariots of the Gods?*

In spite of these and subsequent attacks, von Däniken remained convinced of his discoveries. He refutes his critics and in the preface to a recent edition of his first book maintains his belief that eventually his theories will emerge as the truth.

Von Däniken went on to publish 30 books, many of them best-sellers, translated into some 28 foreign languages. With 62 million books in print, he is one of the most-read authors of all time and he helped to spawn an entire genre of "paleo-contact" non-fiction, including *The Sirius Mystery*. None of his critics, it's worth pointing out, has achieved even a fraction of such notoriety.

Today, von Däniken is a prominent member of the Archaeology, Astronautics and SETI Research Association (AASRA), which publishes new research in the English journal *Legendary Times*. He has given over 3000 lectures in 26 countries and has been the subject of many TV series and documentaries. So successful is the prolific author and researcher that he opened the Mystery Park, a theme park in Interlaken, Switzerland, in 2003. Visitors are invited to walk through themed pavilions to familiarize themselves with ancient mysteries. The park's web site maintains that the exhibits are not intended to present von Däniken's interpretations exclusively, but to inspire curiosity in the wonders of the past.

In July 2004, the Mystery Park recorded its 500,000th visitor. But, like any great monument of civilization, one day it will lay in ruins. And when aliens arrive on earth and discover its rusting hulk millions of years from now, perhaps they'll think of it as we think of Montreal's decaying Olympic Park today—as an unfortunate fad of the 1970s.

Joan Grant
"FAR MEMORY"

*Each [incarnation] has a soul, a personality if you pre-
fer the word. The sum total of all these souls is the spirit
they share between them. The soul usually becomes part
of the spirit after the body dies...When I am doing far
memory, all I do is become aware of the spirit.*

—Joan Grant

Reincarnation is the idea that a person's spirit leaves the
body at death and is later reborn in another. In some
Indian religions, the state of one's soul at death can determine whether it will pass from a higher to a lower life
form, such as a human becoming a snail, or the reverse.
Reincarnation can be put to many uses. It can inspire
belief in the immortality of the soul, connecting souls in
an everlasting cycle, but it can also be used to justify the
unfairness of present reality or to lay blame on past lives
for personal shortcomings.

English author Joan Grant took the concept of reincarnation in a new direction by writing popular books based
on the lives of her previous selves. The jury is still out on
exactly how she did it, but there's no denying that her
work presents, in vivid detail, the lives of historical persons from around the world.

Joan Marshall was born in 1907 into a wealthy English
family. Her father was a tennis champion and scientist; for
many years he was the world authority on the British

mosquito. Her mother purported to have some gifts of foresight.

Joan had many horrifying dreams during World War I. In some, she was a Red Cross nurse tending to casualties; in others, she was a soldier knee-deep in freezing mud of the trenches. All afforded her glimpses into the lives of others.

When she was nine, Joan explained one of her dreams to a soldier who was staying at the family home. She said that she had been in the presence of a man named McAndrew, who had been killed in battle. She provided a description of his regimental badge and used a popular slang word for the trench where he had been stationed. The soldier, dumbstruck, looked into her claim, discovering that the regiment was Canadian and that a man named McAndrew had indeed been killed only hours before the girl described her dream.

As a teenager, Joan was introduced to psychic research by one of her father's friends. But she often felt apprehensive about her unsettling dreams, so she tried to suppress them. A meeting with the writer H.G. Wells, when she was 15, encouraged Joan not to disregard her gift. "Keep it to yourself, Joan," he said, "but never let yourself forget about it. And when you are ready, write what you know about…"

In 1927 Joan married Leslie Grant, a barrister. According to Joan, Leslie's mother had appeared to her in a dream with instructions that she look after him and Malcolm, his twin brother. The couple struggled to make ends meet, especially after the birth of a baby girl in 1930. Joan supplemented their income with odd jobs and also tried to write a book, but abandoned it after she was told

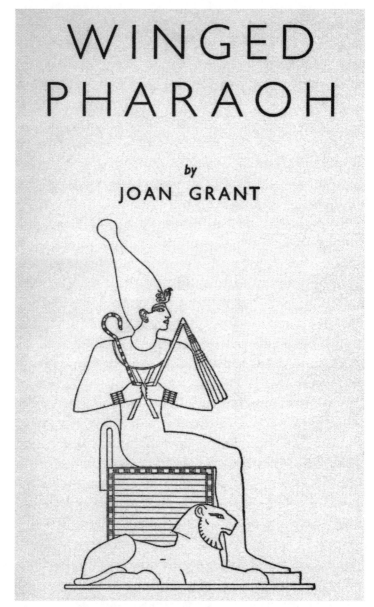

WINGED PHARAOH

by
JOAN GRANT

Title page of Joan Grant's first book, based on her reincarnation as a powerful ancient Egyptian woman named Sekeeta it showed no promise. Constrained to a housewife's role, she focused her energies on her vivid dreams, which were occasionally clairvoyant. She also practiced psychometry, or becoming aware of the psychic energy invested in objects.

Leslie soon abandoned his legal career to join an archeological expedition to Iraq in 1936. Although he had no experience whatsoever as an archeological photographer, he and Joan set off. She intended to use her talents of psychometry on archeological artifacts.

During a vacation in Egypt, the couple visited the ruins of a palace that Nefertiti had once used as a retreat. Joan was overcome with feelings of familiarity; she was uncannily in touch with her surroundings. Then the feelings faded. A few days later, a friend gave Joan some Egyptian scarabs. When she placed one on her forehead, she saw pictures from a young Egyptian girl's life. The girl was Sekeeta, the daughter of a pharaoh who trained for 10 years to become a "winged pharaoh" or priestess and leader. Part of her mystical training involved learning about deaths from previous lives so she could comfort the dying.

Upon returning to England, Joan focused on using what she called "far memory" to relive the events in Sekeeta's life. During 100 or so sessions, in which she rendered herself into a waking trance, Joan vividly described these events. She felt she was not merely seeing Sekeeta's life pass by, but that she *had been* Sekeeta.

Leslie wrote down every detail from the sessions. When Joan was done, they sent the manuscript out. Editors were impressed by the detail, and became convinced that Joan had described lived experiences. Reading very much like a historical novel, *Winged Pharoah* was published in October 1937. Like Joan's subsequent books, it was a success, although the publicity surrounding it ultimately led Leslie and Joan to divorce.

Life as Carola (1939), Joan's next "autobiography," was also composed using far memory. Carola was the illegitimate daughter of an Italian nobleman. She ran away with some traveling performers and learned to play the lute. A man named Carlo di Ludovici, who later became her husband, took her in after she had been abused in a convent. Their happiness was cut short by his death in hunting accident; Carola died soon after in 1537.

Five more autobiographies followed, written with the aid of Joan's second husband Dr. Charles Beatty, a psychologist. Some characters were ancient Egyptians, like Sekeeta and a contemporary of the pharaoh Ramses II, but others were from different cultures, such as a female North American warrior and a priestess from an ancient Greek mystery cult. Most of Joan's previous lives were dramatic and ended graphically—one was burned at the stake, another asked to have her wrists slit.

Grant was not only an author. With her third husband Denys Kelsey, a psychiatrist with an interest in hypnotherapy, she helped patients to determine whether certain memories were fantasies or genuine recollections of past lives. The pair also offered therapy for neuroses and phobias. Joan attributed her own lifelong fear of snakes, for instance, to the death of two previous incarnations from lethal snake bites.

Over the years, Denys and Joan concocted elaborate theories on the nature of reincarnation. They explored in detail the process involved—exactly how one soul re-enters the world in another person, and how the experiences of the past lives can be relived in the present. Using her ideas, Joan even came up with an explanation for ghosts. She thought ghosts were created when a single soul failed to incorporate itself into its greater spirit after death. In essence, she saw ghosts as lost fragments of single souls, which could only be freed through psychotherapy.

What can we make of Grant's remarkable lives and literary accomplishments? For starters, most of what we know about her comes from her current-life autobiography, *Far Memories* (1972). Joan's husbands supported her psychic work, and no one conducted parapsychological investigations of her past lives. We must take Joan at her word, using her books as the only evidence of her reincarnated selves.

Of course, the books themselves are not entirely free of doubt. Even if we concede the existence of Joan's past lives, how exactly these lives were presented in her books is another matter entirely. Why, for example, do Joan's characters lead dramatic lives and die in graphic ways? Isn't it just as likely that previous lives would be more mundane, providing for less entertaining but more believable narratives? It is also curious that Joan's characters cannot be traced through historical records. Like it or not, one must entertain the possibility Joan made everything up. The level of detail in her books runs against this conclusion, so it might be possible that Joan used her past lives as inspiration but embellished significantly.

Another interesting question raised by Joan Grant's life concerns hypnosis and memory. Can a person in a

trance-like state recover past lives or suppressed memories? Probably not, although the idea sounds enchanting
and has many adherents. Witness the rise in "created
memory" experiences, such as UFO abductions, unfounded
accounts of child abuse and encounters with angels. Under
the right conditions, it has been shown that the mind can
create certain memories to fit desired outcomes. If Joan
Grant wanted to become a popular and successful writer,
it's possible her mind could have created her past lives.

William Blake
"I HEARD AN ANGEL"

I traveled through a land of men,
A land of men and women too,
And heard and saw such dreadful things
As cold earth wanderers never knew.

—William Blake, *The Mental Traveller* (*c.* 1810)

Artists lead shitty lives. Many can't afford haircuts, let alone mortgages, new cars and private schools for their kids. Banks withhold credit, and gallery owners are fickle, driven by the vicissitudes of the market. Many of these drawbacks, however, fail to dissuade the determined ones. They are happiest looking at reality in new ways and creating art that reflects their unique vision.

Imagine, if you will, not only a penniless artist, but one whose interpretation of reality was colored, even dependent, on mystical visions. Although cursed to toil without recognition during his life, his visionary work found an audience long after his death, and today he occupies a secure position among the highest rank of English poets.

William Blake was born in 1757, the son of a London hosier. The second of five children, William was a lonely child with a brilliant imagination, and he enjoyed roaming along ditches around London and among its industrial brick kilns. His first vision came at age 10 when he saw angels in a tree as he walked around Peckham Rye. His father was upset when Blake related the incident, and

Portrait of William Blake by Thomas Phillips

only through his mother's intercession did he avoid a thrashing. Another vision came when he saw "angelic figures walking" among hay gatherers in a field. These visions, often with Biblical overtones, recurred throughout his life, and he never ceased to believe in their reality.

Blake was enrolled in a drawing school at age 10. There he learned to sketch the human figure from plaster casts and models of antique sculpture. His ability to render the human body from a classical perspective became a hallmark of his subsequent work. His father supported Blake's training and wanted him to study under a prominent painter, but the family could not afford it. Instead, an engraving apprenticeship was chosen as the next best thing. In 1772, when he was 14, Blake joined the studio of James Basire, engraver to the Society of Antiquaries.

As an apprentice, Blake performed menial tasks and very little of the actual engraving. For the most part, engravers were merely craftsmen, requiring little or no creativity. One of Blake's lasting contributions was uniting the creation and production of own his art into a single process.

One of Basire's projects required Blake to sketch the tombs of kings and queens in Westminster Abbey. Blake gained a great appreciation for the Gothic architecture and worldview, which sharpened his interest in English history and legend. These, along with his affection for Renaissance artists such as Dürer and Michelangelo, helped to form his artistic sensibility. These artists modeled their work on sculptured nudes, preferred Biblical or religious subjects and defined their style with solid outlines, not extravagant colors. Unfortunately, these tendencies were considered bland and outdated by Blake's contemporaries.

After seven years in Basire's shop, Blake possessed the practical skills he would need for the rest of his life. But he still desired to be a painter. In 1779, the 21-year-old was admitted to the prestigious Royal Academy of Art, founded by the famous British painter Sir Joshua Reynolds. Covering his tuition with engraving commissions from book publishers, he prepared himself for a career as a painter, working from nudes and sculptures. Eventually some of his paintings of historical subjects were exhibited. But his unusual style was at odds with the academy's. When one of his senior instructors advised him to study fashionable painters instead of the "stiff" and "unfinished" works of Raphael and Michelangelo, Blake replied, "These things that you call finished are not even begun."

In 1782 Blake married Catherine Boucher, the illiterate daughter of a market gardener. The couple moved into a house near London's Leicester Square. Not only did Blake teach his wife to read and write, he also trained her in printmaking and engraving. Although their marriage produced no children, it was by all accounts very happy, and Catherine stood behind her husband through long stretches of poverty and failure.

Blake was a poet as well as an artist, and his reputation today rests principally on his poetry. In 1783 he published his first collection of verse, *Poetical Sketches*. Composed of lyrics written between the ages of 12 and 20, they showed Blake's unique influences and his great promise. The poems were deceptively simple, almost child-like, and concerned pastoral and industrial subjects. Published with the aid of John Flaxman, a prominent neoclassical sculptor, the book went utterly unnoticed at the time. Blake was soon invited to mix with prominent artists, thinkers and philosophers. He was unimpressed with their company, and later wrote an unfinished lampoon of high society and its manners entitled *An Island in the Moon*.

After Blake's father died in 1784, he set up a printing shop with the aid of a friend named James Parker, a fellow Basire apprentice. The venture folded after four years. During this time, Blake's brother Robert fell ill. Before his death in February 1887, Blake remained devotedly at his bedside for two consecutive weeks. When he died, Blake claimed to see "the released spirit ascend heavenwards, clapping its hands for joy." His exhaustion was so great that he was said to have slept for three days and three nights. But the brothers' contact did not end: Blake continued to see him in visions, and a year later Robert appeared to him and instructed him in a new way of making books. Called "relief etching," it was a bold new process.

Using an acid-resistant varnish, Blake painted the text and the image on to a copper plate. When he immersed the plate in acid, the non-treated parts of the plate were eaten away, leaving only the raised design. Blake could then print each design on to paper using a press. When he had printed all the pages, he and his wife would paint each one with watercolors, trim them and bind them into what he called "illuminated books" or "prints." These resembled the elaborately illustrated hand-drawn books of the medieval era.

Four of Blake's most famous works, including his most well known, the *Songs of Innocence* (1789), were produced by relief etching. Because each copy was an original, the print run was extremely limited. This factor ultimately ensured that only a small minority would read his work, and that mainstream recognition would elude him during his life. Of course, Blake could have had his poems printed traditionally, but he believed in his revolutionary method would make waves, and because he controlled every step of the production, he avoided the censorship and bias he associated with more traditional publishing.

Blake's art was greatly influenced by the Bible and prominent Christian authors. In some works he discussed the creation of the universe, in others his take on original sin and the possibility for redemption. The characters in his later works are mythic, symbolic creatures with names like Urizen, Nobodaddy and Los, not unlike similar ones in the work of the epic poet John Milton, whom Blake greatly admired.

But Blake's idiosyncratic religious beliefs were greatly at odds with any established Christian denomination. In 1789 he attended a meeting of the Swedenborgian New Jerusalem Church, although he never joined and later opposed the Swedish mystic. Still, Blake found a kindred spirit in Swedenborg: both conversed with spirits and had visions, and both believed that extraterrestrial realms such as heaven and hell were extensions of human desires. More importantly, both men were largely misunderstood by their contemporaries, who considered them either mad or deranged.

Blake also opposed the scientific discoveries of the day. He counted among his greatest enemies Francis Bacon, John Locke and Isaac Newton, today considered key figures in the history of science, whose discoveries helped to propel the Enlightenment in Europe. In place of the reasoning faculty they championed, Blake worshipped an imaginative faculty he called the "Poetic Genius." Even his idea of perception differed radically from his contemporaries. He once wrote, "Man's perceptions are not bounded by organs of perception. He perceives more than sense (though ever so acute) can discover." His illustrated books offered a glimpse of a world different from the ordinary one, yet filled with all its political and moral questions. Readers ignored it because it could only be perceived through Blake's unique mythology, cast more in the apocalyptic language of prophecy than any conventional genre of literature.

Meanwhile, Blake struggled to gain recognition. Moving back and forth from the country to London, he depended on a number of patrons and book publishers for commissions. Some of the work involved engraving literary works, both historical and contemporary, but a lot of it was much more trivial. On several key occasions he was promised large commissions, involving hundreds of designs for engraved books, but his patron either handed the work to another artist or went out of business before paying him. After the French Revolution began in 1789, work became increasingly hard to find. The combination of poverty, unemployment and lack of recognition made Blake a bit cantankerous.

In 1803, while he was living near Sussex, Blake's temper got him in trouble. He caught a soldier urinating in the garden, and threw him out by force. The soldier claimed Blake uttered the seditious words, "Damn the king! The soldiers are all slaves." At the time, these were serious words, almost like spouting off pro-terrorist sentiments today. Blake was ordered to appear before a judge. Before the trial took place in 1804, the Blakes moved back to London. Fortunately, the charges were dismissed.

Blake continued to struggle, although he never abandoned his artistic vision. In 1809, he chose to exhibit his work in his brother's hosiery shop, unable to afford to rent space in a gallery. This show was anything but a success. Few came; those who did reacted unfavorably. One critic even suggested that the artist should be locked up, describing Blake as "an unfortunate lunatic whose personal inoffensiveness secures him from confinement."

Blake hit a new low by 1810. Work was nowhere to be found and he felt cheated by his patrons. Then, when all had seemed lost, he fell in with a group of young admirers who supported his work, including John Linell and John Varley, two young watercolorists. Varley commissioned Blake to create a series of "spiritual visitants," based on Blake's visions. The most famous of these is the bizarre "Ghost of a Flea," a remarkable work that could only have been created someone with a capacity to imagine a different world. Linell, meanwhile, secured commissions for Blake to illustrate a number of literary works, such as Dante's *Divine Comedy*. Feeling renewed and appreciated, Blake worked until he fell ill in 1827. With his beloved wife at his side, he died in peace shortly after, at age 69.

One observer said that near the end he continued to describe "the things he saw in heaven."

Blake's reputation ballooned in the 20th century. Some prominent artists and critics, including the Irish poet W.B. Yeats, began to see the remarkable order in his visionary prophetic works. Today he is regarded as one of the great poets of the Romantic period. Although the New Age Blake presaged never materialized, some of the themes he discussed, such as the tensions between the imaginative capacity and free love as opposed to reason and morality, have enjoyed new relevance. If his poetry is better known than his art, it may be on the strength of its magical innocence. In spite of all his troubles, Blake never abandoned his belief in his visions, and he never lost the ability to see the world with the freshness and the clarity of a child.

Hélène Smith
THE MARS WITHIN

*Dodé né ci haudan té méché métiche Astané ké dé
mé véche.*
"This is the house of the great man Astane whom
thou hast seen."

—Transcription of the Martian
language heard by Hélène Smith

The dream of landing a spacecraft on another planet
became a reality in the summer of 1976, when Viking 1 and
2, both designed by NASA, touched down on the red
planet. Since then, many rovers and landers have collected
information on the geology and weather of Mars. Using
parachutes and special airbags, the 1997 Pathfinder craft
landed in area called Ares Vallis, thought to have been a
floodplain long ago. Based on the rover's excavations, along
with other data, scientists speculated that Mars was once
warm and wet, with a thicker atmosphere and liquid water.

None of the missions, however, has turned up any evidence of life or the conditions necessary for life as we
know it. Composed mostly of self-sterilizing dry soil and
saturated with intense ultraviolet radiation, Mars is basically a galactic desert with frigid temperatures averaging
−64° F. Its unlivable atmosphere, made up almost entirely
of carbon dioxide, is subject to nasty dust storms that can
envelop the entire planet. Still, scientists remain opti-
mistic about the planet's past, especially in light of recent

research on "extremophiles," or organisms that can live in highly inhospitable environments such as polar ice caps or near molten-hot volcanoes. But without evidence of liquid water, either on the surface of Mars or below, they must face the disappointing conclusion that the Earth's closest next door neighbor has no alien life forms.

In the late 19th century, a medium named Élise-Catherine Müller, better known as "Hélène Smith," drew a very different picture of the red planet. During her galactic séances, she came across Martian beings, architecture and technology, and even made drawings of her visions. She might have been acclaimed as a brilliant medium had it not been for the research of one inquisitive psychologist, who explained her visions with remarkable psychological insight. Still, her case presents fascinating instances of astral traveling, speaking in tongues and mediumship—and suggests that the unexplored regions of the human mind can be just as fascinating as the empty galactic expanses revealed by multi-mullion dollar space exploration.

By the time of Smith's Mars visions, she had been a medium in Geneva, Switzerland, since the beginning of 1892, with experience in telekinesis, apports and fortune-telling. Her gifts were evident early in life, and may have been passed on to her by her mother and grandmother. Unlike other mediums, Smith did not charge for her services; for many years she held an important position in a silk shop, which allowed her to support herself and her parents. Her atypicality was summed up in a description offered by Théodore Flournoy, who later wrote a ground-breaking book about her:

a beautiful woman about 30 years of age, tall, vigorous, with hair and eyes almost black and a fresh, healthy complexion, which at once evoked sympathy. She evinced nothing of the emaciated or tragic aspect which one habitually ascribes to the sybils of tradition, but wore an air of health, of physical and mental vigor, very pleasant to behold.

Flournoy, a psychologist at the University of Geneva, had followed Smith's activities for several years. Wanting to use the latest psychoanalytical methods to study her, he asked to be invited into her circle and was admitted in 1894.

At a séance in November 1894, Smith found herself floating through space. She landed in a distant land, revealed as Mars by her guide, which she proceeded to describe in acute detail. Smith said the Martians were like humans, but shorter, usually less than three feet tall, with small heads and eyes but gigantic mouths. They glided around on wheel-less carriages powered by emitting sparks and lived in houses with fountains on the roofs. One description even included an early version of a jet pack, at least 50 years before it entered the vocabulary of science fiction:

On the bridge there was a man of dark complexion carrying in his hands an instrument somewhat resembling a carriage lantern in appearance, which, being pressed, emitted flames, and which seemed to be a flying machine. By means of this instrument the

man left the bridge, touched the surface of the
water and returned again to the bridge.

Smith, who later became an artist, made drawings of
the flowers, people and houses she saw on Mars. Most
remarkable of all, Smith's guide taught her to speak the
Martian language, a sentence of which is quoted at the
beginning of this account. This phenomenon, sometimes
called speaking in tongues or xenoglossia, involves the
ability to speak in a language completely unknown to its
user, often prompted by an otherworldly source.

Upon further investigation, Flournoy met Smith's spirit
guide (and guardian angel), "Leopold," a pseudonym for
the infamous alchemist Cagliostro. Announcing himself to
Smith through raps, automatic writing or incarnation, he
oversaw séance activities, answered questions put by Smith
and facilitated contact with distant locales and persons
from history. Smith's manner changed drastically while
under Leopold's influence. She spoke with a thick Italian
accent, assumed a more confident, even brash personality
and wrote in a hand very different from her own.

Leopold claimed that he had resurfaced because he
still sought the company of Marie Antoinette, the illustri-
ous yet doomed queen of France in the 18th century, with
whom he was hopelessly infatuated. Smith, who offered
descriptions of Marie Antoinette's life and surroundings,
claimed the dead queen was one of her earlier incarnations. Another historical persona who spoke through
Smith was a princess named Simandini, the daughter of
an Arab sheik who lived 500 lives previously. Most
remarkable of all, Simandini had married a lover from a

past lifetime called Prince Sivrouka—whom Smith identified as Flournoy!

The professor was flattered by this detail and intrigued by Smith's bizarre visions, but remained unconvinced about her mediumship. By exploring her past, Flournoy soon uncovered very realistic sources for her often supernatural capabilities.

Flournoy learned that Smith's father, a merchant of Hungarian extraction, had a knack for languages and was fluent in a handful of European dialects. Even though his daughter spoke only French and a little bit of German, she had heard many languages spoken around the house, so it was quite possible that sounds from various languages had been combined, unconsciously, to form the Martian dialect, whose grammar was basically French. Subsequent investigation has shown that 98 percent of the words that she claimed were alien could be traced back to human words.

Flournoy also noted Smith's inability communicate in Italian while under Leopold's guidance. That seemed strange, since Cagliostro was born and raised in Palermo. While under his influence, Smith used a foreign accent, but this accent was not genuine evidence of xenoglossia. Leopold additionally offered obscure answers to questions about his life; he produced not a single tangible fact. Flournoy was forced to conclude, against popular opinion, that Leopold was a second personality of Smith's, not a real person. He existed in large part to act out or disguise conflicts from her personal life, past and present. This notion was highly original at the time, not least because many psychologists of the era were keen observers of séances and mediumship, and therefore not convinced of their invalidity.

Still, some aspects of Smith's mediumship baffled Flournoy. During the first séance he observed,

> I was greatly surprised to recognize in scenes which passed before my eyes which had transpired in my own family prior to my birth. Whence could the medium, whom I had never met before, have derived the knowledge of events belonging to a remote past, of a private nature and utterly unknown to any living person?

He also failed to examine in any detail Smith's earlier acts of physical mediumship.

Flournoy's findings, the fruit of five years of research, were published as *From India to the Planet Mars*, which was lavishly praised as a brilliant work of psychology upon its publication in 1899. Smith was unimpressed. She felt Flournoy's behavioral approach did little justice to the mysterious nature of her gifts, especially since some of the reviews of the book had ridiculed her mediumship. She banned Flournoy from attending future séances and refused to be studied again.

Yet Smith reaped some of the rewards of Flournoy's work. She was beset with letters and requests for séances, making her an overnight celebrity. An American benefactress even granted her a salary for life, allowing her to leave her job. Smith also demanded royalties from the book sale, and Flournoy granted her half; the other half he donated to the local psychology archives.

Until her death in 1929, Smith traveled to celestial bodies such as Uranus and the moon, but with decreasing frequency. Her certainty about her own powers was unchanged and could invariably be traced to her multiple personalities. In 1903, she had a vision of Christ and was told by Leopold, "You will draw Him." Never marrying, she spent the latter part of her life painting pictures of religious subjects. None of these images—which seemed mediocre, almost unworthy of the subject that inspired them—were ever displayed or sold. Near the end of her life she told an interviewer:

> I am not someone who loves to exhibit her-self. I do not wish at any price to be a subject. I have…suffered too much, been too mal-treated because of this gift of mediumship, which I did not seek out.

In late 19th-century France, Mars was a fashionable distraction. An astronomer named Schiaparelli had dis-covered canals on the planet in 1877, while *The Planet Mars*, a book by the famed French astronomer Camille Flammarion, became a popular best-seller in France. Although Smith was the most prominent Mars traveler, several other persons also stepped forward with claims to have made contact. Far from being coincidental, their astral voyages seem to indicate an important fact about paranormal phenomena: they are often psychological and inspired by real events or the fantasies of popular culture, especially those engulfed in a cloud of mystery. Today, because we know a lot more about the red planet, cases of astral trips are uncommon. UFO sightings, on the other hand, which are not well understood, continue to occur. Théodore Flournoy deserves recognition for his careful investigation of Smith's case. Unlike other skeptics, he did not deny the existence of mediumship, nor was he obsessed with exposing Smith; he sought only to understand her.

It's worth quoting his assessment of Smith's case because it could easily be applied to many persons in this book: "a case of idealism against grey reality...On the wings of a dream, the individual flies, hoping to escape the thousand and one discouragements of the prosaic everyday."

3
Insightful
Skeptics

Houdini
CONTRA SPIRITUALISM

*...after more than thirty years' experience in the realm
of mystery, I can truthfully say that I have never seen a
mystery, and I have never visited a séance which I could
not fully explain.*

—Houdini, 1922

Houdini remains the greatest conjurer of all time. The
writer George Bernard Shaw once observed that the three
best-known names in history were Jesus Christ, Sherlock
Holmes and Harry Houdini. Though the golden age of
conjurers has past, he remains the subject of countless
books, films and television programs, and many of his
famous escapes still remain cloaked in mystery.

Late in Houdini's career, after he had traveled the globe
and made his fortune, he worked to expose spiritualist
mediums. His various attempts to reveal their schemes
weren't always fair or successful, and they seemed to point
to two sources of vulnerability: his dead mother and the
rigidity of his beliefs.

Ehrich Weiss was born in 1874 in Budapest, Hungary,
the son of Jewish Hungarian immigrants. After the family
moved to Appleton, Wisconsin, his father struggled to
make ends meet as a rabbi. Later the Weisses moved to
Milwaukee and then to New York City, where Ehrich tried
to pursue a career in vaudeville while working in garment

Houdini (seated, left) rings the bell with his foot under the table while pretending a spirit makes "contact."

factories. The young conjurer, who could pick all the locks in his house as a small boy, showed remarkable gifts.

In our technological society, it's hard for us to imagine the rise of vaudeville in the late 1890s. Back then, radio, film and television did not exist for popular consumption. Masses of people crowded into public theaters to witness the fabulous talents of conjurers, acrobats and freaks who traveled across the globe. Few became great successes, but those who did were adored everywhere.

Ehrich chose the stage name Harry Houdini. "Harry" was probably derived from "Ehry," a nickname his beloved mother had given him, while "Houdini" was taken from Ehrich's idol, the French conjurer Eugène Robert Houdin. Ehrich assumed, mistakenly, that adding an "i" to the name would mean "like Houdin." Later, Houdini would unfairly criticize his former hero in a book entitled *The Unmasking of Robert Houdin.*

Houdini married Bess Rahner in 1894, and she became his assistant. The pair performed magical tricks, false acts of telepathy and escape routines, but struggled to make it in America. In 1900, they set off for Europe, where Houdini first earned international acclaim by escaping from a Siberian prison van in Moscow.

Houdini's fame grew during the early years of the 20th century. Contrary to popular belief, he was not the world's greatest magician. His reputation rested mostly on his incredible escapes from every conceivable contraption—boxes submerged in rivers, straitjackets, bank vaults, coffins. A clever self-promoter with a sizable ego, Houdini often caused a stir wherever he performed; his confident personality and enormous appetite for publicity were as much a part of his act as his astounding feats.

Houdini's mother Cecilia died in 1914 while he was away in Europe. Her death had a profound impact on the conjurer, leading him to explore the possibility of survival after death. Many spiritualist mediums of the time promised to contact dead loved ones, so Houdini began to attend their séances.

He became convinced that the spiritualist mediums were fakes, intent on bilking the public with false promises of contacting dead loved ones—much in the manner of "Crossing Over" medium John Edward today. Drawing on his enormous library of paranormal books and his extensive experience as a performer, Houdini set out to expose the false mediums, staging his own demonstrations of

Late in life, Houdini performed entire shows to expose the fakery of mediums.

"unfakable" séance phenomena such as psychokinesis (moving objects with the mind) and spirit manifestations. In so doing he earned the enmity of spiritualists everywhere.

Houdini's unusual friendship with Sir Arthur Conan Doyle, the creator of Sherlock Holmes, became a focal point of his debunking activities. Houdini had met Doyle, one of his heroes, in London in 1920. The two were polar opposites: Doyle was convinced Houdini's powers had a psychic source, while Houdini insisted that it was all trickery. Still, they became fast friends.

A rift arose in 1922, when Doyle's wife, a noted medium, conducted a séance in Atlantic City to contact Houdini's mother. Using automatic writing, Mrs. Doyle went into a trance and wrote out a letter in English from Cecilia Weiss. Houdini refused to believe it; his mother spoke only German and Hungarian. Nor did the spirit medium's vague generalizations about his mother being happy in the afterlife impress Houdini. The Doyles, on the other hand, considered the séance a complete success, claiming that the supposed inconsistencies were irrelevant in the séance setting.

Houdini's most controversial case took place in 1924. The year before, in the pages of the magazine *Scientific American*, he had promised $5000 to anyone with bona fide proof of mediumistic powers. Later, unbeknownst to the conjurer, a panel of experts from the magazine considered offering the prize to a Boston housewife and medium named Mina Stinson Crandon, a.k.a "Margery."

An incensed Houdini rushed to Boston to sit in on the séances and discredit Margery. Although it remains unclear exactly what happened, the two parties were very distrustful of each other. Houdini even set several traps— and was caught red-handed.

During one of the séances, Margery was asked to ring a bell that was inside a box. Walter, her spirit control, quickly accused Houdini of rigging the bell so it couldn't ring. When the bell was inspected, it became clear that a

Houdini took aim at "spirit photography" with this staged image, in which the "ghost" of Abraham Lincoln appears beside the escape artist.

piece of rubber had been wedged near it, preventing it from ringing. Walter complained again when he sensed that Houdini had planted a ruler in the box in another attempt to frame Margery. Houdini's assistant later admitted that he had requested this ruler be placed in her box so it could be used against her.

By the end of the episode, Houdini was unable to present any damning evidence; all he could summon was a plea for a more demanding test. Although Margery was never awarded the money and was later exposed, the case was perceived as a defeat for Houdini. His stubborn ego had gotten the best of him.

In 1926, the year of his death, Houdini was invited to testify in front of the U.S. Congress. The government was considering a law that would have forced fortune-tellers to earn a license to practice their craft. The skeptical Houdini recommended that the laws be toughened because the proposed license would lend legitimacy to fortune-telling. When asked if he himself had paranormal powers, Houdini offered a vehement denial. About his escape routines, which the mediums claimed involved psychic powers, he said, "I do it like anybody else would do it. There is nothing secret about it. We are all humans. Nobody is supernormal. We are all born alike."

After Houdini's death, many spiritualists, including Conan Doyle, proclaimed that the conjurer had used psychic powers. How else to explain his seemingly impossible escapes or his ability to stay enclosed in a box underwater for more than an hour? While these speculations interested a baffled public, they ignored one pressing question. If Houdini did in fact have special powers, as they claimed, why on earth would he expend so much energy exposing mediums and even publishing books such as *Miracle-Mongers and Their Methods* (1920) and *A Magician Among the Spirits* (1924)?

The last straw was connected to Houdini's final challenge to the mediums, made shortly before he died. He said that if survival after death was in fact possible, then he would communicate a coded message to his wife after he passed away. He offered $10,000 to any person who could intercept this message from the beyond. For her part, Bess held a séance every year on the anniversary of his death in the hopes of contacting her husband.

In 1929 a medium named Arthur Ford gave Bess Houdini what he thought was the mystery message:

"Rosabelle believe." "Rosabelle" was a pet name Houdini used for his wife, and the message was set in a special code used by the Houdinis in their early vaudeville acts. When Bess signed a document, witnessed by a reporter, attesting to the veracity of Ford's message, the public was astonished.

But not for long, as it turned out. It later emerged that Bess had tipped off Ford beforehand about the contents of the message. Bess denied the leak, and Ford and the reporter made their own statements and accusations. As in the Margery case, confusion reigned, but one thing was clear: Houdini had not communicated a message from the beyond.

So what can we conclude about Houdini? It's likely that he harbored some hope of survival after death, as evidenced in his attempts to contact his deceased mother, but his performer's ego prevented him from allowing the mediums of the day to conduct what he thought were bogus séances. On at least one occasion, it led him to cheat to prove his point. Whether he cheated in his dealings with other mediums is uncertain. Either way, Houdini's infamous reputation remains intact.

Some conjurers who succeeded Houdini took up his interest in exposing paranormal fakery. Following a successful magic career, James Randi (a.k.a "The Amazing Randi") became a prominent anti-paranormal author, and even imitated Houdini's offer of cash to anyone who could prove, under controlled conditions, that paranormal powers exist. The weakness of these skeptics is often their vehement and even emotional denials of any genuinely inexplicable phenomena.

James Randi
SKEPTIC EXTRAORDINAIRE

Peter Popoff was a prominent televangelist. Back in the early and mid-1980s, at the height of his popularity, his ministries collected money primarily through mail solicitations. In his book *The Faith Healers* (1987), prominent skeptic James Randi estimates that Popoff sent out as many as 100,000 letters every week from his headquarters in Upland, California. Popoff's mailing list, provided by scam artist "Reverend" Gene Ewing, included names of persons known to contribute to religious causes; Popoff added other names through his television and radio spots. The letters themselves, also the work of Ewing, were worded so as to make a donation seem imperative to offset an imminent crisis. There seemed to be a crisis every month.

The ploys were ridiculous but remarkably effective. Popoff would send out objects such as "golden prosperity envelopes," blessed shoe liners and even a scraps of hankies anointed with his sweat; supporters, feeling blessed and content to make a difference, would send in a donation. In 1985 Popoff pleaded for funds so he could arrange to have Russian-language Bibles dropped in the Soviet Union via balloons, ostensibly to convert the godless communists from their wicked ways. It was like an evangelical Marshall Plan.

Then, to raise even more money, a few Popoff cronies broke into the ministry's warehouse and printing facility, made a mess and soaked about 10,000 religious brochures

James Randi, former conjurer and head of the James Randi Educational Foundation in Florida

with hoses. A TV crew taped Popoff's sorrowful reaction to this rigged spectacle the next day, with tears courtesy of a cut onion. With his wife Liz at his side, the preacher blamed "Satanists and secular humanists" who had destroyed 100,000 of the Russian Bibles intended for his divine mission in the USSR, adding that he would use his own money to cover the damage to his facilities. Then, pleadingly, he asked his followers to pitch in.

How much money Popoff took through this and other scams is unknown. Under law, televangelists are only required to report personal incomes, not total donations received. It's safe to assume he obtained many hundreds of thousands, even millions of dollars, all tax-free.

One woman in Chicago donated her life's savings, some $21,000. When she asked for a portion of it back, Popoff's people refused. The same fate awaited a woman from Welland, Ontario, who had started giving to Popoff in 1980. As the need escalated, she drained her savings, borrowed from relations and later a bank to raise the cash—in total, about $13,000. When her family found out, they urged her to approach the ministry to get some of the money back. No response, no refund.

The mailing list was Popoff's best source of revenue, but his sermons provided seemingly incontrovertible evidence of his miraculous healing powers. During the preacher's early years, he displayed no supernatural powers, relying on the tricks of other TV evangelists and faith healers. But somewhere along the way, Popoff became able to "call out" the names and addresses of total strangers in the audience and even "see" their illnesses. This gift, and his ability to heal the afflicted, were thought to come by way of a divine "gift of knowledge." Congregants would swoon as people were called out, making individuals more prone to feel healed when no such healing had taken place.

Skeptics, led by Randi, were not convinced. Randi had first discovered the scam while attending a Popoff event in

Texas with Steve Shaw, a member of the Houston Society to Oppose Pseudoscience. To expose the chicanery, the skeptics falsely answered personal questions and provided made-up information on the so-called "healing cards" passed out before the event. If Popoff called out any of their false data during the sermon, Randi and his team would know that he was receiving the information not from God or a supernatural source but by some other means. This didn't happen, but the investigators came across a key piece of information when Shaw got close to Popoff and noticed an electronic device in his left ear.

Randi needed definitive evidence before he could expose the evangelist. Alec Jason, an electronics specialist and member of the Bay Area Skeptics, helped him get it during a Popoff appearance in San Francisco in 1985. Using a sophisticated radio scanner, Jason was able to tune into 39.170 megahertz, God's direct line to Popoff. Only it wasn't God giving the preacher the details, it was his wife, Liz. Before the event began, Jason recorded the following clip:

> Hello Petey, I love you. I'm talking to you. Can you hear me? If you can't, you're in trouble 'cause I'm talking. As well as I can talk. I'm looking up names right now. I forgot to ask, are you going to preach first or minister first. Heeelllloooo! I love you.

Liz proceeded to give the names and address of sick people in the audience. Popoff, of course, made it seem like this information, along with the sufferers' ailments, came to him from God. Subsequent recordings showed that Liz Popoff and others often poked fun at the obesity, poverty and gullibility of the congregants.

With all the evidence he needed, Randi appeared on *The Tonight Show* with Johnny Carson in February 1986. At first he presented a 60-second clip from a Popoff event in Anaheim as it had appeared on television. Then the clip was shown again, this time dubbed over with Liz's voice delivering information to her husband. The audience was shocked, as was Johnny Carson: the evidence came through loud and clear.

Popoff's ministry struggled in the wake of the Randi exposure, especially since it took place on one of America's most popular TV shows. Although the preacher was forced to concede the use of what he called a "communicator," he refused to admit to his duplicity. He threatened to sue Randi but never did; in fact, he eventually laid people off and had to re-envision his ministries. But almost as if to prove the public's blind faith in televangelism, even in the wake of such a definitive expose, Peter Popoff is back on TV and in the mail, only now he also uses a slick web site.

Perhaps this unfortunate development speaks more than any other to the necessity of paranormal skeptics. James Randi remains the world's most famous. The author of 10 books, the white-haired crusader has published articles in *Time, Scientific American, Encyclopedia Americana* and the *New York Times,* to name only a few. Along with countless television spots, he has appeared at the White House, the Smithsonian Institution and at famous universities around the world. In 1986, in recognition of his efforts in alerting the public to hoaxes and pseudoscience, the MacArthur Foundation of Chicago awarded Randi its prestigious $272,000 prize.

Today, Randi is the head of the Florida-based James Randi Educational Foundation (JREF). Founded in 1996, the non-profit organization began with a sizable donation from an anonymous IT magnate. The JREF is basically an information source for students, media, researchers and the merely curious. The foundation boasts more than 300 members, sells merchandise online and participates in skeptical congresses wherever they are held.

Randi is a funny, sharp man with a stern look and a white beard. Although he has worked with the media for much of his life, he believes that it helps to foster belief in paranormal phenomena. He argues that journalists, who are mostly educated in the humanities, not the hard sciences, often lack the wherewithal or patience to test paranormal claims with any kind of rigor. Yet they and their editors realize that paranormal stories capture the public interest. If, for instance, an aircraft disappears in the Bermuda Triangle, it might be reported prominently, as if to confirm the mysterious nature of the storied zone. Yet no follow-up coverage will appear when the missing persons or parties turn up again. Randi argues that cold, hard facts, often based on long scientific studies, are less interesting to read than gripping stories of disappearing aircraft, UFOs from outer space and people with psychic powers.

Randi's role as a respected watchdog of paranormal fads is well known. In 1999, he appeared before the U.S. Congress to discuss homeopathy, much as Houdini had appeared before Congress in 1926 to warn about fortune-tellers. Proponents of alternative medicines such as Andrew

Weil had become famous by touting nontraditional approaches to medicine and pharmacology. With his flair for the dramatic, Randi took 32 times the recommended dose, proving the ridiculous levels of dilution in homeopathic drugs. He suffered no ill effects, and concluded that the drugs were ultimately ineffective and that homeopathy was quackery.

Also like Houdini, Randi was a famous conjurer before he set out to expose paranormal fakery. Born Randall James Zwinge in Toronto, Ontario, in 1926, he was a shy, awkward kid with unusually high intelligence and a voracious appetite for knowledge. When he skipped school to see a performance by Harry Blackstone, Sr., a famous magician, he found his calling.

He dropped out at 17 to join a traveling road show as Prince Ibis, a wise wizard in a turban. Later he adopted the name "The Amazing Randi" and built a reputation performing levitations, escape routines and sleight of hand. He appeared before royalty in Asia and in Europe, on college campuses across North America and on a number of television specials, including *The Tonight Show*.

Along the way, Randi came across many psychics and charlatans who used conjuring methods to perform supposedly paranormal feats. Incensed by this fraud against the public, especially in cases where money was involved, he set out to expose the fakery whenever it existed. But he quickly realized that many people believe and support utter nonsense, regardless of evidence to the contrary. Arguably the best example involves crop circles in Great Britain. In 1991, Doug Bower and David Chorley admitted to making approximately 250 circles, providing a convincing explanation of how and why they created the puzzling designs. Remarkably, many people continued to believe that the circles had otherworldly origins, and were coded with Sumerian symbols or patterns of alien DNA.

To combat this kind of blind faith, Randi has staged many convincing, irrefutable exposés that enraged people in the paranormal community. His techniques, highly reminiscent of Houdini's during his debunking period, differed greatly from those of parapsychologists of the past and present, whose pseudoscientific methods and findings helped to lend credibility to some psychics and clairvoyants without any hard evidence.

In 1976, Randi helped to found the Committee for the Scientific Investigation of Claims of the Paranormal, a Buffalo, New York–based organization. Its mandate, in brief, was "to examine [paranormal claims] openly, completely, objectively and carefully" and publish findings in its magazine *The Skeptical Inquirer*. Among CSICOPs members were many renowned professors, scientists and Nobel laureates, as well as colleagues or friends of Randi such as the author Martin Gardner and the legendary astronomer Carl Sagan.

CSICOP was instrumental in helping Randi pursue charlatans such as Peter Popoff, as well as psychic surgeons, water diviners, astrologists and others. One of his most successful exposures was of Israeli spoon-bending celebrity Uri Geller. In the late 1970s, Geller was set to appear on *The Tonight Show* to determine, using his psychic gifts, which of three metal canisters contained water. Before the show, unbeknownst to Geller, Randi painted rubber cement on the bottom of the canisters. When

Geller "mistakenly" bumped the table to see which canister didn't slide and therefore held the water, none of them moved. Flustered, the psychic floundered on stage during this stunt and others, then claimed that he was ill and couldn't perform.

But Randi's extended exposé of Geller, *The Magic of Uri Geller* (1975), was far from perfect. Among other fallacies, Randi claimed that Geller had been "tried in a court of law and convicted" for fraud in Israel. This statement was untrue, as were others made in the book. The public battles between the two men became increasingly bitter: one would make a brash statement in a magazine, then the other would counter with an equally venomous rebuttal.

CSICOP's board members, meanwhile, advised Randi to back down, fearing the financial ramifications of legal action from Geller. Randi refused and left the organization in 1992. In total, Randi has been sued by his nemesis half a dozen times and by others as well. He lost only one case, but his legal fees have consumed much of his MacArthur Foundation grant. But, like anyone who's convinced of his vocation, he takes the loss with a grain of salt.

To his credit, Randi does more than simply criticize. He urges those with paranormal claims to approach the JREF and have their claims tested. The reward is the "One Million Dollar Paranormal Challenge" and is offered to "anyone who can show, under proper observing conditions, evidence of any paranormal, supernatural or occult power or event." According to rules posted on the JREF web site [www.randi.org], the foundation does not carry out the testing itself; it simply sets out, in collaboration with the applicant, the conditions under which the test will take place.

The conditions named for this test—easily the most lucrative of its kind—have invited criticism, like so much of Randi's work. Opponents say that Randi reserves too much power to oversee the test conditions of any proposed paranormal feat, and that the lack of an independent judge means that only the JREF's approval will grant the prize. These criticisms appear unfounded. In spite of many attempts, no one has won the prize, which is made up of negotiable bonds held in a Goldman Sachs vault.

A more serious criticism of Randi's work has often been leveled at CSICOP. It goes that the skeptical position unfairly presupposes the nonexistence of paranormal phenomena and is therefore untenable. Randi denies this criticism, reiterating his lack of preconceived notions. He claims, for instance, that he cannot openly deny the arrival of Santa Claus every Christmas Eve, although all the evidence to date seems to speak against it. Paranormal claims deserve a similarly open-minded treatment.

Still, there's no denying Randi's bitter and often cynical tone, often in evidence on his weekly web site newsletter *Swift*, where his manner is curt. In the preface of one of Randi's own books, Carl Sagan described him as "rambling, anecdotal, crotchety and ecumenically offensive." Although the JREF operates, like its predecessor CSICOP, with an open-minded mandate and is willing to test claims before offering judgment, Randi clearly has a tacit opposition to all claims to the paranormal, if not any specific naming of such. And while he's generally justified in his remarks, especially given the amount of fraud perpetrated by charlatans and mountebanks, much of what Randi targets is *not* fraudulent or harmful per se; it's just a stubborn man trying to be right at all costs.

Given Randi's outlook, we may wonder what he might make of miracles such as the incarnation and resurrection of Jesus Christ or similar unexplained events from other world religions, often cast in the form of stories from holy texts. If these phenomena defy validation by skeptical criteria, is it worth jettisoning religious belief in favor of a more scientifically verifiable code of conduct? After all, many people give generously to churches all over the world, sometimes in the millions of dollars, so it may appear that a scam is being worked on them. Perhaps the mystery of the unknown, often at the heart of any religion, is as compelling as anything that human ingenuity can explain.

In the end, it falls to each individual to decide. Randi's contributions to the paranormal debate are remarkable, especially for a self-educated expert without scientific training, but the fact remains that many sane and rational people believe strongly in the power of suggestion, sixth sense and meaningful coincidences, and will continue to do so. As the upcoming chapter on paranormal charlatans shows, it's unfortunate that some have used this wonder to exploit the unsuspecting.

Reginald Scot
WITCH HUNT CRUSADER

My question is not, as many fondly suppose, whether there be witches or not; but whether they can perform such miraculous works that are imputed to them.

—Reginald Scot, *Discovery of Witchcraft* (1584)

Today's skeptics disavow belief in the paranormal to protect the public from being fleeced. The targets of their attacks are invariably those who profess to have paranormal abilities when none exist. During the witch craze in Europe, the opposite was true. Skeptics aimed to protect innocent people with no paranormal powers from accusations of practicing witchcraft or consorting with the Devil. Their efforts, unfortunately, were not entirely successful: for nearly 250 years, starting in the middle of the 15th century, historians estimate that between 150,000 and 200,000 witches were executed.

The majority, nearly 100,000, came from Germany. One of the most horrendous cases involved the Pappenheimers, a vagrant family from Bavaria that scraped by cleaning privies and begging. Anna and Paulus were the parents of three sons, Michel (also known as Jacob) and Gummprecht, both in their 20s, and a 10-year-old called Hänsel. It's worth recounting their story to illustrate the shocking levels of unfairness and cruelty involved in the witch hunts.

In February 1600, when an accused thief named them as accomplices in the murder of a pregnant woman, all the adults in the family were hauled from their beds and imprisoned. Hänsel was left behind at first; later, at a loss at what to do with him, the authorities reunited him with his family in prison. Although the Pappenheimers initially declared their innocence, they all broke under torture, confessing to witchcraft and human sacrifice. Incredibly enough, their troubles had only started.

Duke Maximilian I of Bavaria, eager to make an example of the family, had them transferred to Falcon Tower, a dungeon in Munich. There they were subjected to extreme torture, including *strappado*, one of the more common scourges. With little choice, the family offered more confessions, and they were taken before a judge for sentencing.

The list of crimes was ridiculous. Unsolved murders were dredged up and other crimes were invented to increase the severity of the punishment. Paulus' crimes, according to the official accusations, included using sorcery to cripple or slay 100 children and 10 adults, stealing from churches, killing 44 others, arson, robbery and burglary. The others received similarly exaggerated lists of crimes; all, with the exception of little Hänsel, were sentenced to death. In the end, after a horrifying punishment that included many forms of extreme torture, the whole family was burned at the stake.

The Pappenheimer case remains one of the most repulsive on record. Although it was atypical in its cruelty, its scapegoating tactics, forced confessions and elaborate pageantry of cruelty linked it to witch trials across Europe.

Many factors fueled the European witch craze, including the desire of the Catholic and Protestant churches to persecute heretics. Other factors included unpredictable crop failures and plagues, for which responsible parties were sought, often out of revenge, and the misogyny of the church against women, who were thought weak and susceptible to temptation by the Devil.

Another factor, often underrated, was the key role played by anti-witch books. Between the 15th and the 17th centuries, the power of the printing press grew exponentially. Unlike our own time, when books are plenteous and tend to disappear as fast as they arrive, the books of the Renaissance and Reformation could exercise a powerful influence over long swathes of time. The pope in Rome supervised the interpretation of the most important book, the Bible, and enjoyed the authority to censor banned books (Protestants took great issue to both these points). He could also lend the church's *imprimatur*, or seal of approval, to legal and political tracts.

One such book was the *Malleus Maleficarum* or "The Witch Hammer." First published in 1486, it served as a comprehensive guide for inquisitors. Its authors, Heinrich Kramer and James Sprenger, were empowered by Pope Innocent VII to persecute witches in Northern Germany. Papal authorities felt the civil courts were not punishing witches in great enough numbers, and a definitive manual would serve to quell Protestant opposition to the Inquisition.

Kramer and Sprenger argued that God opposed witches in the scriptures, so it would be heretical to deny the existence of witchcraft. They affirmed the existence of the Devil and his witches, attributing to them a variety of abilities, including disrupting fertility, transforming into animals and tempting humans with incubi and succubi. To illustrate their points, the authors drew far-fetched examples of human sacrifice, copulation with devils, spells and Satanic pacts from the literature of the Inquisition.

The final section of the *Malleus* was a kind of "how to" manual. It advised how to try, sentence and execute those guilty of practicing witchcraft. The solicitation of confessions was a key point, since the authors believed that "common justice demands that a witch should not be condemned to death unless she is convicted by her own confession." To exact confessions, torture was considered entirely justified, and was urged for those who refused to confess voluntarily.

The influence of the *Malleus* was profound. Published in dozens of editions across Europe, it was considered an indisputable authority for more than 200 years. Montague Summers, a famous witchcraft historian, offered the following assessment in a 1948 edition of the book:

> The *Malleus* lay on the bench of every judge, on the desk of every magistrate. It was the ultimate, irrefutable unarguable authority. It was implicitly accepted not only by Catholic but by Protestant legislature. In fine, it is not too much to say that the *Malleus Malleficarum* is among the most important, wisest and weightiest books in the world.

Until the publication of Paul Bunyan's *Pilgrim's Progress*, it was probably the best-selling book in Europe apart from the Bible. Scores of well-educated men, including the influential French scholar Jean Bodin, endorsed its claims, well aware of the inhumanity it recommended. Bodin thought that anyone who denied the existence of witchcraft was himself a witch and deserved the same punishment.

To speak out against the witchcraft described in the *Malleus* was risky, but not unknown. In 1563 a German doctor named Johann Weyer attacked the inquisitors in his book *De Praestigiis Daemonum*. He believed that Satan acted alone in promulgating witchcraft; the women accused were almost always innocent victims. Frauds who tried to cast spells or use magic should be punished, he wrote, but anyone who repented should be forgiven. For a while, Weyer's efforts were successful in discouraging witch hunts in the Netherlands. Unfortunately, his opponents in the church and among royalty reacted venomously, causing witch persecutions to become even more severe.

Another witch skeptic, a Jesuit, spoke from his own experience. Johann Spee became a confessor in Würzburg, Germany, during the height of the witch trials in Bavaria. Like many in his position, he believed earnestly in the threat of witchcraft and the persecution of heresy. But as he received the confessions of the condemned, he became increasingly revolted by the torture and collusion used against innocent victims. With even the slightest hint of an accusation, a witch was condemned and almost always expected, under torture, to name accomplices. There was simply no hope of a fair trial: regardless of how the accused behaved, whether she lived or died under duress, the accusation of witchcraft stuck and a death sentence was inevitable.

Spee published a pamphlet, *Cautio Criminalis*, in which he denounced the inquisitors and revealed their duplicitous methods. He was correct to point out a financial incentive behind the hysteria, since bonuses were awarded on the numbers of witches burned and the inquisitors could confiscate the belongings of the condemned. Like Weyer's, Spee's publication was initially condemned as heretical. It was later translated and circulated across Europe, although its influence was negligible.

Among English writers on the subject, Reginald Scot stands alone. Neither a clergyman nor an academic, he remains one of the greatest skeptics in the history of the occult. His book did not so much save lives as courageously challenge an entire climate of belief.

Scot was born in 1538 to a wealthy family in Kent in southeastern England. Attending Oxford at 17, he left without taking a degree. A bright and sensitive young man, he worked as a subsidiaries collector, served in Parliament and managed his cousin's estate. Although he married in 1558, his wife died, leaving him childless. His interest in hop gardening led to his first book, *The Hop Garden*, in 1574.

Witch hunts were much less severe in Great Britain than on the Continent; the worst occurred in Scotland. In North America, in places such as Salem, Massachusetts, they were even less pronounced. Nevertheless, Scot's indignation at the irrationality of the witch craze, along with his witnessing of a mass witch trial in a nearby town, inspired him. He immersed himself in all the demonological literature, both for and against, as well as folklore and legal cases. He was heavily influenced by Weyer, although his stance was much stronger because of his Protestant leanings. The result of his voluminous research, *The Discovery of Witchcraft*, was published in 1584.

Taking aim at the *Malleus* and "the extreme and intolerable tyranny" of the Inquisition, Scot advanced a relatively simple thesis: no woman accused of witchcraft had supernatural powers. Only God wielded such powers, not humans or witches or even the Devil. He admitted the existence of malevolent witches, but advanced that they harmed people with poisons, not by any occult means. Like Weyer, he described the typical witch as a blameless middle-aged woman, often poor or of low intelligence, who became a scapegoat for local superstitions or the object of revenge. Another category of witches was deluded mental cases, who convinced themselves of a pact with Satan when none existed. A final group of women were simple opportunists who made money selling witch's spells, prophecies and curses. None of these women had powers of any kind, regardless of what they were made to confess.

Scot described witchcraft as a "cozening art"—similar to magic insofar it was based on illusion. Part of *The Discovery of Witchcraft* was devoted to revealing, years before Penn and Teller, the secrets of conjuring tricks, from sleight-of-hand to coin and ball gaffs. The same skepticism was applied to spells, ghosts, omens, fairies and other topics now considered folkloric. As evidence, Scot tried to invoke spirits himself and met with no success.

Scot also challenged questionable Biblical interpretations used to persecute witches. A famous example was the Witch of Endor, who was said to have raised Samuel from the dead in the Old Testament. At the time, many scholars considered her a necromancer and a predecessor of modern-day witches; some even said that she conjured the Devil, not Samuel. Scot, on the other hand, presented the conjuration of Samuel as a hoax, in keeping with many of his theories about contemporary witches. If demonologists used the Witch of Endor to justify the persecution of witches, he argued, they had incorrectly interpreted scripture or were twisting it to their own ends.

The Discovery of Witchcraft would have enjoyed greater popularity had it been published in Latin instead of English. King James, however, was violently opposed to the book, and had his own refutation published. The rumors that he had copies of Scot's book burned appear untrue. Regardless of its influence, it remains a heroic document, and Reginald Scot deserves recognition as an important predecessor of today's paranormal skeptics.

4

Paranormal Pioneers

Charles Fort
COLLECTOR EXTRAORDINAIRE

Nothing is real, but that nothing is unreal; that all phe-nomena are approximations one way or the other between realness and unrealness.

—Charles Fort, *The Book of the Damned* (1919)

Near the end of the film *Magnolia* (1998), thousands of frogs suddenly fall from the sky. The amphibian hailstorm breaks windows, terrifies motorists and even prevents a TV quiz show host from killing himself. What's so remarkable about the scene, other than its appropriateness in an intense film about Los Angeles, is that this kind of thing really happens.

Reliable observers have reported falls not only of frogs, but of fish, snakes, birds, worms and other creatures, according to William Corliss in his book *Handbook of Unusual Natural Phenomena* (1976). Though scientists readily admit that these occurrences are not imagined, they have struggled to explain them. Why, for instance, does the transporting mechanism often select only one species and fail to deposit sand or other debris? Or why do saltwater species of fish, only found in deep water, fall from the sky during freshwater storms? Prevailing theories point to weather phenomena such as waterspouts and whirlwinds, but they fail to cover the diversity of the phenomena in question. Scientists are left with more questions than answers.

A master collector of inexplicable phenomena, Charles Fort never found recognition in his life.

Their confusion would have delighted Charles Fort. The eclectic writer was obsessed with falling objects, among other things, and he became the first to list and speculate on related phenomena in rigorous detail. Although Fort carried his obsession with the uncanny a little too far, he remains a paranormal pioneer, and a healthy reminder that some commonly observed phenomena (by which I do *not* mean UFOs) simply defy rational explanation.

Charles Fort was born in Albany, New York, on August 6, 1874, the first of three sons. His mother died when he was four, forcing his father to raise the brood with the family housekeeper. Charles' father, from a family of successful Dutch grocery wholesalers, was very strict, and he often beat the boys or imprisoned them in a dark room for days at a time. This experience led to Charles' subsequent distaste for authority and dogma, mentioned in several passages of *Many Parts*, the author's fragmentary autobiography.

Fort was a difficult yet observant boy who liked to collect biological specimens. Though he never did well in school, he showed great promise as a writer; by age 17, he had published stories in the *Albany Democrat* and the *Brooklyn World*. He ran away to New York City at 18, hoping to make it as a journalist, then traveled to England, Scotland and Africa. To support himself, he wrote travelogues and did odd jobs. When he contracted malaria in South Africa, Fort was forced to return to New York, where he met up with Anna Filan (or Filing), a servant girl in his father's house who he had known for nearly a decade. They were married on October 26, 1896.

For years, the penniless couple lived in tiny apartments in the Bronx. Fort continued to write for newspapers and magazines, but many of his stories, now lost, were rejected. His only other sources of income came from menial jobs and a rental property in Albany he had inherited from his grandfather. Anna was a sociable housekeeper who never had the first inkling about Fort's unusual work. The sturdy-looking Fort, on the other hand, was unusually asocial in spite of a remarkable sense of humor. An odd couple, no doubt, but nevertheless a good match according to those who knew them.

In 1905 Fort met Theodore Dreiser, an editor who published some of his stories in *Smith's Magazine*. Dreiser was himself a talented novelist; his novel *Miss Carrie* (1900), initially published to little acclaim, went on to become one of the great novels of American letters. One of Fort's only friends, Dreiser admired his fiction and acted as his agent, but none of Fort's 10 novels, apart from the unsuccessful *Outcast Manufacturers* (1909), were ever published.

When one of Fort's uncles died in 1916, the 42 year old received a generous inheritance. He could finally quit his career as a journalist and devote all his time—some 27 years—to collecting anomalous information. To this end, he and Anna moved London in 1921 to have access to the British Museum's vast collections. They later returned to New York, where Fort was a fixture at the New York Public Library for many years.

Fort combed through popular and scientific journals during the day, making careful notes about unusual phenomena, then pored over them during the evenings. His massive collection of note cards was kept in a wall of shoeboxes in the Fort residence, where Fort occasionally had visitors over to drink his homemade beer. As a writer, Fort was prone to fits of depression and doubt, and twice burned tens of thousands of notes in frustration. But like any determined intellect, he soon picked up the torch again, having learned his lesson.

Over the years, Fort's notes were incorporated into four fascinating books upon which his reputation rests: *The Book of the Damned* (1919), *New Lands* (1923), *Lo!* (1931) and *Wild Talents* (1932).

These books are basically eclectic compendiums of anomalous observations. The first two focus on Fort's favorite topic, falling objects such as unusually colored rains, frogs, fish, slabs of ice and even fossils. Fort also explores mysterious airships (later called UFOs), flashing lights and earthquakes. *Lo!*, his third book, introduces Fort's most original concept, teleportation—the mysterious removal of an object from one place to another. (Fort would have been appalled at the uses put to this concept by New Agers and by Gene Roddenberry, creator of *Star Trek*.)

Fort's final work, *Wild Talents*, published right before his death, presents more human mysteries—unexplained disappearances, kidnappings and spontaneous human combustion. "Wild talents" such as witchcraft, dowsing and stigmata are also discussed.

What was Fort's take on his material? None, really. Anti-dogmatic in the extreme, he refused to adopt a rigid scientific perspective—or any other, for that matter. Instead of explaining the phenomena he collected in a rigorous way, he simply listed them and speculated how these "damned" data were excluded from science. He never hesitated, however, to make some pretty unusual observations of his own, many with more poetic merit than factual consistency. Take the following passage on "blood rains" from *The Book of the Damned*:

> ...our whole solar system is a living thing...showers of blood upon this earth are its internal hemorrhages—or vast living things in the sky, as there are vast living things in the oceans—or some one especial thing: an especial time, an especial place. A thing the size of the Brooklyn Bridge. It's alive in outer space—something the size of Central Park kills it—it drips.

Fort readily admitted that some of his interpretations were unsatisfactory, but the best available given the bizarre data under consideration. Fort's weirdest creation might have been "the Super-Sargasso Sea," which hung like a heaven over the earth. Living things originated here, and intelligent beings periodically let these living things fall to earth, in part to communicate with secret societies below.

How serious was Fort? Not very. Much of his approach was tongue-in-cheek; after all, he wasn't trying to "prove" his interpretations in a traditional way as much as to single out instances that left science in the dark. Not that he was an expert in the latter: although his curiosity was bound-less, Fort's scientific training was somewhat limited. He also neglected to check the reliability of his sources. Not all journals and newspapers are equally reliable, but Fort often assumed that because something appeared in print, it merited insertion into one of his books.

Still, numerous organizations and periodicals have grown up around Fort's work. While he was still alive, a disciple named Tiffany Thayer founded the Fortean Society. (The withdrawn Fort, who admitted to Dreiser he wanted nothing to do with the venture, had to be surreptitiously lured to the inaugural gala. He was convinced that such a society would attract only weirdos and spiritualists.) After Fort's death, Thayer selected material from his remaining notes and began publishing it in the *Fortean Society Magazine* (later called *Doubt*).

Today, the most popular Fortean publication is the always fun yet not always serious *Fortean Times*, although many others continue to explore the bizarre, including *INFO Journal*, published by the International Fortean Organization, and magazines such as *Strange* and *The Anomalist*. Each of these publications spins the anomalous data in its own way: some make use of true science (such as William Corliss' *Science Frontiers*), while others, almost blind to developments since Fort's time, speculate wildly on UFO abductions and other dodgy phenomena.

Skeptics are many. About Fort, James Randi, the famous paranormal debunker, wrote:

> ...his books serve to illustrate how outlandish and highly improbable claims, made along-side a small percentage of genuinely true but incredible events, can capture the imagination of the public.

Hard scientists take a similar tack, lending little credence to Fort's vacuous "intermediatist" position, which
held that nothing was unreal and nothing was real. What
these skeptics can't dismiss are the small numbers of genuinely baffling phenomena that Fort identified.

If Fort's life and work proved anything, it's that inexplicable events are regularly documented and deserve our
attention. Even if we lack the appropriate framework to
grapple with them, they can be mind-expanding and sub-
versive. At the limits of scientific knowledge—a remote,
unpredictable place where anything is possible—the seeds
of imagination can find purchase. And some laughs too.

Eileen Garrett
LIFELONG JOURNEY

I have a gift, a capacity—a delusion if you will—which is called "psychic." I do not care what it may be called, for living with and utilizing this psychic capacity long ago inured me to a variety of epithets—ranging from expressions almost of reverence, through doubt and pity, to open vituperation. In short, I have been called many things: from a charlatan to a miracle woman. I am, at least, neither of these.

—Eileen Garrett, *Adventures in the Supernormal* (1949)

Irish-born Eileen Garrett failed to enjoy the popularity of other mediums, but her tireless search for answers about her own mediumship, which had roots in her own troubled life, made her one of the most respected paranormal personalities of the 20th century.

Eileen's life was full of tragedy. Her mother was Irish and her father was a Spanish Basque, and they had married rather suddenly abroad. Upon their return to Ireland, Anne's rigidly Catholic family ostracized them because her new husband was a Protestant. Their only child, Eileen Janette, was born on March 14, 1892, in County Meath. Anne soon drowned herself, and her husband took his own life six weeks later. The child was rendered into an aunt's custody while still an infant.

In one of her autobiographies, *Adventures in the Supernormal* (1949), Eileen characterized her aunt much like a spiteful stepmother—a woman who had no patience for the imaginative fancies of an isolated little girl. Eileen grew to hate her, even as a young child. Once, in an odd yet fitting act of revenge, the little girl killed some ducklings that she saw in the woods near her house. She later felt terribly ashamed.

Alienated from her family and schoolmates, Eileen was most content to spend time alone with "The Children," a group of imaginary friends consisting of one boy and two girls. They shared her powerful connection with the natural world:

> …they loved everything that grew and flowered, and they opened up my sense of beauty. They shared my enthusiasm for the garden and the fields; every stone had a story, every hill in the neighborhood had an adventure for us. Trees and shrubs became our friends.

As Eileen spiraled into a self-created world, her unusual sensitivity led her to see "surrounds" or auras around all living things. The communication among such beings was often wordless, which had significance for her subsequent interest in mediumship:

> …it seemed that I knew what the flowers and trees were saying without the use of words. Even today, words have not the value to me that others place on them…The inadequacy of words, to express emotions, thoughts and feelings has, from time to time, created a barrier

between me and others, and even made it seem impossible for me to explain myself and my method of functioning to most other people.

Eileen was prone to respiratory sickness for much of her childhood. At 15, she left Ireland to stay with relations in the drier climate of London. She soon fell in love with a charming older man, an architect called Clive Berry, and they were married. Eileen became pregnant four times, losing three sons shortly after birth; only a daughter, also named Eileen, survived. Berry had been unfaithful from the start, and the couple divorced after he began living openly with another woman. It was the first of several failed marriages.

Eileen found work at a hospital for convalescent soldiers during World War I. There she met her second husband, who was killed when he returned to the front. Now ill again, Eileen met a third husband, J.W. Garrett, who was also a soldier. This marriage also failed in short order, leaving her with only his last name. Fortunately, Eileen's nascent interest in séances and other spiritualist activities, which enjoyed unprecedented popularity after the war, gave her a new focus.

A pivotal moment came in 1920s. Eileen was at a table-tapping session, i.e., a meeting in which sitters communicate with the dead through a table's movements. Initially indifferent to the proceedings, she fell asleep and began muttering about dead relatives of those gathered around the table. When Eileen awoke, feeling nauseated and woozy, those around her told her what had happened.

To learn more, and against her husband's advice, Eileen consulted a theosophist name Mr. Huhnli. Under his guidance she descended into a deep trance and communicated with her first "control":

> On my awakening, the teacher informed me that he had spoken to one "Uvani," an entity or control personality of Oriental origin, who foretold that I would become the vehicle for this type of work and that for a number of years I would serve in the capacity of trance medium.

Although "Uvani," who Garrett claimed was an Arab soldier from the 14th century, became her most noted medium, others emerged over the years, including a 17th-century Persian magician called "Abdul Latif." He later became a focus for messages about healing.

Eileen's reputation as psychic, trance medium and clairvoyant grew under the tutelage of Dr. James Hewat McKenzie, a Spiritualist at the British College of Psychic Science. Until his death in 1929, he was pivotal in honing her gifts, although the two disagreed over the nature of her powers. While McKenzie believed that Uvani was a separate entity, Eileen was convinced he was a part of her subconscious, who spoke to her through mediumship. She described her controls as "principles of consciousness" that grew out of her emotional needs.

Any doubts about Eileen's powers were dispelled in October 1930. The British airship *R101* had crashed on October 5, 1930. Two days later, while Eileen was in a trance at the National Library of Psychic Science, the ship's captain, Flight Lieutenant H.C. Irwin, communicated through her, offering a detailed account of the tragedy, including a dangerous gas leak. This communication was taken down and submitted to the Air Ministry. Officials were shocked when some of the technical details in her account closely matched those in the official report published a year later.

Eileen moved to America in 1931, accepting an invitation from the American chapter of the Society for Psychical Research. She repeatedly offered to have her gifts tested by parapsychologists. In the 1940s, she visited Duke University in North Carolina to participate in experiments conducted by Dr. J.B. Rhine, a parapsychology pioneer who invented the term "extrasensory perception" (ESP).

Rhine and one of his colleagues, Dr. Karl Zener, had developed cards for use in experiments with telepathy, precognition and clairvoyance. The deck consisted of 25 cards and had five symbols: a star, a cross, a square, a circle and three wavy lines. Without being able to see the cards, subjects were expected to identify them psychically. (The opening minutes of the film *Ghostbusters* present a funny parody of these experiments. Dr. Peter Venkman, a parapsychologist played by Bill Murray, falsely congratulates a beautiful undergrad for her remarkable ability to guess the right cards, while offering electric shocks to a hapless male counterpart, who actually guesses several cards correctly.)

Volunteering was a risky move for Eileen. For the most part, mediums had participated exclusively in experiments conducted by "pet" scientists, i.e., those who would guarantee positive—or at least inconclusive—findings.

Rhine's methods, while not entirely scientific, were more charlatan-proof than others. Eileen's results were only slightly better than average, as were her results in other tests. But she didn't mind: understanding was her goal, not fame or money.

Eileen Garrett was much more than a guinea pig. An astute businesswoman and prolific writer, she eventually built up a small publishing empire. Her most notable magazine venture, *Tomorrow*, was a literary and political magazine whose contributors included Thomas Mann and Robert Graves; in the 1950s, it shifted its focus to psychic subjects. Some of Eileen's books, among which *The Sense and Nonsense of Prophecy* (1950) and *Adventures in the Supernormal* (1949) are probably the best known, were published by Creative Age Press and Helix Press, her own imprints. She was also the subject of several books, including Allen Angroff's *Eileen Garrett and the World Beyond the Senses* (1974), which made a careful analysis of her different spirit controls.

Eileen's greatest accomplishment may have been her founding of the Parapsychology Foundation in 1951. While serving as its president, she raised money for research (even from a Republican congresswoman from Ohio), organized many important conferences and published a newsletter and a prominent parapsychology journal. At the time few universities were willing to hold conferences on parapsychology. When she died in September 1970, in Nice, France, Eileen was mourned by many in the paranormal community.

Eileen Garrett's life recalls Joan Grant's. Both survived lonely childhoods filled with strange visions, and both later found a home in the paranormal that neither family nor marriage could offer. But because Eileen was somewhat mystified by her abilities, and became convinced that her controls emerged from her troubled subconscious, she seems more genuine than Joan, who concocted many purportedly scientific theories about reincarnation. More importantly, Eileen's search for answers about herself contributed immeasurably to research being done by others—no small feat in the relatively new and highly contested field of parapsychology. If Eileen Garrett is little known today, it's probably because popular interest in parapsychology has all but disappeared.

Bernard Heuvelmans
THE FIRST CRYPTOZOOLOGIST

Cryptozoological research should be actuated by two major forces: patience and passion.

—Bernard Heuvelmans, 1988

Apart from its proximity to Christmas, December 23, 1938, was like any other day. Hendrick Goosen, a South African fisherman, went out on the waters of the Indian Ocean and returned in the early evening to sell his catch at a fish market near Cape Town. As was his habit, he called Marjorie Courtenay-Latimer, a taxidermist and fish collector from the nearby East London Museum, to see if she'd like to pick through his haul. Courtenay-Latimer did, not finding much of interest, and was about to leave when she spotted an unusually reflective fin. She pulled the other fish aside to reveal a bizarre, beautiful specimen, some five feet long and measuring 127 lbs. It had rolled oversize eyes and unusual fins, and oil had oozed from under its large metallic blue scales.

Rushing back to her museum with the smelly fish, Courtenay-Latimer provisionally identified it as a coelacanth (later named the *Latimeria chalumnae* in her honor), a lobe-finned fish that first appeared on earth 350 million years ago. That in itself was not unusual; many species of fish, such as sharks, have survived virtually unchanged for eons. Paleontologists, however, had assumed that the coelacanth had died off with the dinosaurs. The species was known only through fossil records, and none of these postdated the Cretaceous period some 65 million years ago. So how had one ended up in her hands?

Courtney-Latimer promptly contacted South Africa's leading ichthyologist, J.L.B. Smith of Rhodes University, Georgetown, to confirm her discovery. At the time Smith was away on holiday. Courtenay-Latimer's boss, meanwhile, dismissively identified the specimen as a grouper and left it at that. Upon his return, Smith shared Courtney-Latimer's verdict; he was amazed by the remarkable, even historic, find. Unfortunately, by this time the specimen's fleshy innards, necessary for any kind of indisputable identification, had decayed.

Somewhat like a zoological Captain Ahab, Smith became obsessed with finding another live coelacanth. For 14 years he visited islands in the West Indian Ocean, interviewed fishermen and searched the oceans. Then, while he was on another Christmas holiday, someone else beat him to it.

Transplanted British fisherman Eric Hunt became deeply interested in the coelacanth after attending one of Smith's lectures. On December 21, 1952, as Hunt was returning to the island of Comoros off the coast of Mozambique, he was approached by a man dragging a large catch behind him. Introducing himself as Ahamadi Abdallah, a Comorian fisherman, the fisherman told Hunt that the catch he held was called *gombessa* by his people, and that such fish were occasionally pulled onto local boats. Hunt was ecstatic; he had discovered the second coelacanth. As soon as Smith was alerted, he obtained and preserved the specimen in excellent shape, ensuring that scientists worldwide would recognize it, which they did. (To read the entire story, see Smith's classic book *Old Fourlegs* [1956].)

Over the last 50 years, more than 200 coelacanths have been caught, classified and placed in museums. In 1997 another kind of coelacanth was spotted in an Indonesian fish market almost 7000 miles away from Comoros. Scientists rushed to the area and were able to recover a live specimen. They concluded that the species lives in deep caves along steep inclines near underwater volcanoes—a habitat very similar to the African varieties. Once again, fishermen of the North Sulawesi region had caught the species—called *rajalaut* or "king of sea" —for many years, yet it remained undetected by Western scientists.

So what does the coelacanth reveal about the paranormal? Several important facts. First, it shows that some species may exist undetected, even though zoologists believe them extinct or, as we will see, imaginary. It also shows that indigenous cultures are often familiar with hidden species unknown to traditional zoology. As a result, "cryptozoologists" postulate that fantastic creatures such as the abominable snowman and the Loch Ness monster could just as plausibly be out there somewhere, just waiting to be discovered.

If we continue to believe in this possibility today—and it should be noted that many scientists do *not*—it's largely because of Bernard Heuvelmans. He was the father of cryptozoology, the science that seeks unknown or extinct species or those known only through folklore. Motivated by a passionate desire to extend the limits of scientific inquiry, Heuvelmans opened the way for many follow-ers—including the most prominent, Loren Coleman, on whom I have relied for this account—although few were able to combine the master's well-rounded learning with his surprisingly down-to-earth approach.

Heuvelmans was born in Le Havre, Belgium, in 1916. From a very early age he was interested in animals, espe-cially monkeys. He was also fascinated by the science fic-tion of the day, such as Jules Verne's *20,000 Leagues Under the Sea* and Conan Doyle's *The Lost World*, which he reread many times.

Heuvelmans attended the Free University of Brussels, earning a doctorate by age 23. For his dissertation in zool-ogy, he classified the teeth of the aardvark, which were previously considered unclassifiable. The combination of scholarly acumen and contrarianism would become a trademark of Heuvelmans' manner as a scientist. After graduation he published articles in a variety of journals, including the *Bulletin of the Royal Museum of Natural History of Belgium.*

During World War II, Heuvelmans was conscripted for military service. Repeatedly captured by the Nazis, he escaped no less than four times. To make ends meet, he found work as a jazz singer until he got a break writing a column on the history of science. The job required him to become conversant in all the sciences from a humanistic perspective—a capacity that would serve him well later in life.

After the war Heuvelmans settled in Le Visenet, out-side of Paris. Along with his scientific interests, he pur-sued his passion for jazz and translated several works of zoology, including *The Secret World of the Animals* by Dr. Maurice Burton, subsequently released as the seven-volume *Encyclopedia of the Animal Kingdom*.

Although he showed many talents, no one in particular had brought Heuvelmans acclaim. Then, in 1948, he read an article in the *Saturday Evening Post* entitled "There Could Be Dinosaurs," about the possibility of relict (or surviving) dinosaurs. The author, Ivan T. Sanderson, was a Scottish biologist who had written some popular books about natural history. The article inspired Heuvelmans to focus his energies on the search for hidden species, with the understanding that a traditional scientific approach could not yield all the answers. Over the next five years, and without institutional support for his unorthodox inquiries, he collected sizable "dossiers" of information about unknown land animals from both scientific and folkloric sources.

The resulting book, *On the Track of Unknown Animals*, was originally published in French in 1955; an English translation followed in 1959. Heuvelmans begins his 550-page tome with an invective against the "rash dictum" of Baron Georges Cuvier, the 19th-century scientist who invented paleontology. Convinced that zoologists had already detected all the world's large vertebrates, Cuvier declared in 1812 that "there is little hope of discovering new species of large quadrupeds."

In response, Heuvelmans names scores of large quadrupeds discovered since Cuvier's declaration, including the okapi, the komodo dragon, Przewalski's horse (the last "wild horse"), the pygmy hippopotamus and even the giant panda, which today appears on the logo of the

World Wildlife Fund. These creatures were once thought imaginary or extinct, so their discovery places in question many zoological assumptions, especially in cases where scientists had dismissed the testimony of native cultures as nonscientific.

Heuvelmans spends the rest of the book examining the evidence for unknown species that have eluded discovery, such as the African Nandi bear, the moa of New Zealand (an odd ostrich-like bird), the Patagonian giant sloth, the mammoth of the Eurasian taiga and extant dinosaurians, among many others. If you suspect this amounts to a lot of facts, dates and measurements, consider the following passage, which gives an indication of Heuvelmans' approachable style and his inventive use of sources:

> It is dawn in a small village on the coast of Tanganyika. Suddenly the silence is broken by a woman's shrill scream. On the still-fresh sand in the marketplace lies a shapeless heap of flesh, the unrecognizable body of a man, ripped and pounded to mincemeat by some incredible killing machine. The scavenging birds fly off their carrion, and one by one the villagers gather round in a circle, silent until one of them notices a few grayish hairs among the drying blood and exclaims: "*Mngwa*."
>
> The *mngwa* is the most feared of all Africa's mysterious beasts, although the whites do not know it at all, and even to the blacks it is

largely a mystery; for its name comes from the Kiswahili *mu-ngwa*, which means "strange one." East African settlers often confuse this animal, which the natives call *nunda*, with the Nandi bear. But the terrors of Africa do not come all in one shape. Whereas the *chemosit* is a lumbering beast reminiscent of a bear, the *mngwa* is distinctly feline, a silent machine with muscles like steel springs, controlling an armory of teeth and claws…

Although some might characterize this material as pseudoscience, Heuvelmans' ability to fuse the literary, scientific and humanistic is rare in our culture of research overspecialization.

Heuvelmans devotes much of the book to one of his passions: unknown primates. One of the most noteworthy chapters gathers together all the evidence for the existence of what he called "the not so abominable snowman," including sightings from across southern Asia as well as fake scalps and other false leads. Other chapters dwell on a possible lost tribe of Ceylon and various "wild men" scattered across the globe.

Although it was not the first book of its kind, *On the Track of Unknown Animals* quickly became a popular best-seller. More importantly, it inspired other zoologists to pursue "living fossils." Heuvelmans quickly received a barrage of mail from scientists who shared his beliefs or who had been working in the same vein; many went on to do groundbreaking field research, often in collaboration with the Belgian trailblazer. Even his old mentor Ivan

Sanderson fell under his influence, and later dedicated his classic, *Abominable Snowmen: Legend Come to Life* (1961), to Heuvelmans and his wife, Monique Watteau.

The term "cryptozoology" was not coined by Heuvelmans. That honor fell to a French wildlife official named Lucien Blancou, who dedicated one of his books to "the master of cryptozoology" shortly after the publication of Heuvelmans' landmark study.

His next project, *In the Wake of the Sea-Serpents* (1968), was a counterpart to his first book, which had investigated only land vertebrates. This volume speculated on more than 500 sightings of sea creatures, including sea serpents, giant squids and other oceanic cryptids. Once again, Heuvelmans' style was to combine scientific learning with a sympathetic ear for noteworthy eyewitness accounts.

In 1968, Ivan T. Sanderson invited Heuvelmans to view the so-called Minnesota Iceman, thought to be a frozen cadaver of a hairy hominid recovered from the Siberian tundra. Embracing it as a new species became a source of embarrassment for Heuvelmans after its caretaker, exhibition guru Frank Hansen, informed the media that it was a fake replica. The iceman became the subject of a 1974 book that Heuvelmans wrote with Boris Porshnev. Heuvelmans' other books, as yet untranslated from French, focus on dinosaurs and relict hominids in Africa.

To uphold objectivity in a field that had the potential to attract many pseudo-scientists, Heuvelmans created the Center for Cryptozoology in 1975. Located outside Paris, it held his huge private library and his extensive cryptid files; he also used it to publish the journal

Cryptozoology. In 1982 Heuvelmans became president of the International Society of Cryptozoology in Washington, D.C. He was also involved with the British Columbia Scientific Cryptozoology Club and other organizations. His many honors included a prestigious citation from the Zoological Museum at the University of Hamburg in Germany.

In the last decade of his life, Heuvelmans' involvement in the field he helped to create declined. He refused to be interviewed by the media or for documentaries and his writing activity all but ceased. After years of failing health, he donated his files to the Museum of Zoology of Lausanne in Switzerland 1999, fulfilling a promise made in 1986. Two years later, on August 24, 2001, he passed away in his home in Le Vesinet, France, at age 84. His wife of many years buried him in his Buddhist regalia.

No cryptozoologist after Heuvelmans could match his expansive knowledge of scientific and anthropological sources. He was eager to overthrow orthodox perspectives he believed untrue, yet he never let his personal convictions determine the results of his research. These are qualities of a talented if unorthodox scientist, and that's how Heuvelmans should be remembered.

In spite of Heuvelmans' contributions, cryptozoology is not officially recognized as a branch of zoology and it probably never will be. There are several reasons why. First, any "science" that studies species that *might exist* or exist only through testimonials is not a science. Any way you look at it, the basic requirements of zoological classification have remained the same: living specimens, intact skeletons or other hard evidence. Second, because cryptozoology lacks recognition from the scientific community, many nonscientists have become involved. They range from individuals interested in spotting Bigfoot in the Pacific Northwest to "armchair" experts who have combed all the evidence in print but are not trained to do field research. Many of these cryptozoologists are interested in positive results, and this tends to color their findings.

Perhaps most important, since Heuvelmans' time a fascination with spectacular "Hollywood" creatures, fed in part by the media's sensational interest in the paranormal, has drawn attention away from some of the truly hidden species, such as the coelacanth or the giant panda. Compared with sea serpents and extant dinosaurs, these animals seem less interesting or threatening, but it's important to remember their discovery inspired crypto-zoology in the first place.

A final note. Since the 1960s discoveries of new, non-cryptid animal species (and especially insects) have multiplied. Advanced technologies such as night-vision lenses allow scientists to observe the behavior of previously unobservable nocturnal animals, while other technologies have opened up previously inaccessible habitats, such as the ocean floors and the canopies of dense rainforests. By contrast, the use of similarly advanced technologies to establish the existence of popular cryptids—i.e., the big ones—has produced no comparable results. In fact, intense testing with sonar has all but eliminated the likelihood of discovering creatures such as the freshwater sea serpent in Scotland's Loch Ness. One can only wonder what Heuvelmans would say.

Dr. Franz Anton Mesmer
ANIMAL MAGNETISM

Anyone who has seen Dr. Mesmer at work cannot fail to be impressed by his skill and to marvel how he effects his cures by personal magnetism without magnets.

—Letter from anonymous observer, 1775

Hypnotism seems to produce a state between sleep and waking in which subjects become prone to suggestion. Yet anyone who's seen a hypnotist in action can testify to how difficult it is to determine what's going on. Is the hypnotist a "strong-willed" person? Why are some people more prone to suggestion than others? Finally, how do some subjects become insensitive to pain, recall hidden memories or perform incredible acts of physical endurance under hypnosis? Even today, hundreds of years after its invention, hypnotism is not entirely understood.

What we do know is that it was originally used for therapeutic reasons, and its origins can be traced back to an 18th-century doctor named Anton Mesmer. During the heyday of his miracle cure—called "mesmerism" or "animal magnetism"—Mesmer was a celebrity, the toast of pre-Revolutionary France. And while he did not invent hypnosis, and might seem like an unlikely paranormal personality, his strange work spurred a powerful new interest in the unexplained mysteries of the human mind.

Very little is known about Mesmer's early life. He was born in Iznang, a small German village near Lake

Constance, in 1733. His father was a gamekeeper, and Anton was one of nine children in a devoutly Catholic family. After a relatively uneventful childhood and adolescence, he earned a degree in astronomy in Germany and then tried for a law degree at the University of Vienna, although he soon switched to medicine. Mesmer's practical training consisted of ancient methods such as bleeding, blistering and purging, as well as fashionable new cures such as electrotherapy, in which electrical currents were applied to affected organs.

After six years, he published his dissertation, *De planetarum influxu*, which examined the influence of the sun, moon and tides on the human body. Although it seems ridiculous today, in the 18th century the idea of a single force—or, as Mesmer would later claim, a fluid—that exerts a powerful influence over human health was not uncommon. Mesmer had in fact cribbed much of his work from Richard Mead, an English doctor who had proposed a very similar idea in 1704. Mesmer graduated in 1766 and over the next eight years built up a successful medical practice in Vienna with a list of wealthy patients.

A lifelong music aficionado, Mesmer was an accomplished player of the glass harmonica and was friends with Mozart, Gluck and Haydn. His easygoing, cultured lifestyle was bolstered by his marriage to Anna von Bosch, a rich widow 10 years his senior who had a teenage son. Good looking, with a muscular physique and a slow, deliberate manner, Mesmer was a civilized man with important colleagues.

One of them, Maximilian Hell, a Jesuit priest and advisor to the Austrian Empress Maria Theresa, became interested in magnets after an Englishman named John Canton had learned to forge them artificially from stainless steel in 1750. Magnets had recently been used in England to treat stomach aches and tooth decay, although these "cures" were still unfounded. Hell lent some magnetic plates to Mesmer to try out on one of his patients.

The first recorded cure by way of magnetism came in July 1774. Mesmer's patient was Fräulein Francisca Oesterlin. According to Mesmer's notes, quoted from Derek Forrest's *Hypnotism: A History* (1999), her ailments were many:

> Her hysterical fever caused continual vomiting, inflammation of the bowels, stoppage of urine, excruciating toothache, earache, melancholy, depression, delirium, fits of frenzy, catalepsy, fainting fits, blindness, breathlessness, paralyses lasting some days and other symptoms.

All other treatments on the 28 year old had failed. Mesmer laid the plates on her body. Her attacks, which could last for hours at a time, continued for a few minutes but ceased shortly thereafter. Mesmer returned to treat Oesterlin during subsequent attacks and each time the treatment appeared to work, if only temporarily. The ebb and flow reminded Mesmer of the motions of the celestial bodies discussed in his thesis; in his mind, magnetic attraction and repulsion were not entirely dissimilar. He referred to the universal action of the magnetic fluid on the body as "animal magnetism."

Mesmer suspected he was on to something big, so he invited Anton Stoerck of the University of Vienna to examine his evidence. Stoerck refused, worried that the academy would disapprove. Eventually Mesmer attracted the attention of Jan Ingenhousz, a skeptical Dutch physician from the Royal Academy of Science of London. In what became the first of many dismissals from the scientific establishment, Ingenhousz called the new magnetic cure a ridiculous fraud. Then, to make things worse, Hell came forward and claimed that *he* was the first to suggest the magnetic therapy.

The controversy, from which Mesmer emerged the victor, helped to draw attention to his new treatment, especially after some successful treatments of epilepsy, paralysis and depression. Mesmer's next important patient, no less controversial, was Maria Theresa von Paradis, an 18-year-old piano player who had been blind since the age of four. Paradis was a favorite at the court of Empress Maria Theresa, her namesake, so her progress would doubtless be the subject of parlor room gossip.

The girl's condition wavered dramatically during treatment; at times it seemed she was cured, then she would relapse. Mesmer made a great mistake by inviting Paradis to his home and treating her behind closed doors, allowing his enemies to level accusations of immorality. Soon skeptics from the Faculty of Medicine, including Stoerck, came forward to test the claim. The girl was still blind, and her continued presence at the doctor's home remained a sore point. People wondered why Mesmer's patients were all pretty young girls and why he insisted they dress in loose smocks and have their breasts and thighs kneaded for therapy. Mesmer's medical license was revoked and he left Vienna under a shadow, abandoning his wife.

In 1778 he arrived in Paris and quickly established a *clinique* in his apartment on the fashionable Place Vendôme. By this time Mesmer's method had changed. He had abandoned his belief in the curative power of the magnets themselves after watching Father Johann Gassner, an exorcist who effected "cures" merely by waving his hands over affected areas and staring at patients with his penetrating gaze.

Such "laying on of the hands," of course, has a long history, stretching back to the Bible and is still in use even today. Royalty such as Charles II of England was said to have cured thousands of people with scrofula and tubercular inflammations merely by touches from his divinely sanctioned hands. The practice was called "Touching for King's Evil," and even non-royalty joined in now and then. In the 1600s, the English healer Valentine Greatraks, a.k.a. The Stroker, convinced many people that God had given him the power to cure the king's evil.

Mesmer, however, was not content with a mere laying on of the hands. He wanted to combine a medical ritual with what he believed, quite earnestly, about the potency of the magnetic fluid. His group healing routine became an elaborate, even sorcerial affair, carried out in a setting ideally designed for the decadent world of pre-Revolutionary France.

The showpiece was a large wooden tub, the so-called *baquet*. About 15 feet in diameter and two to three feet deep, it was filled with treated water (containing iron, stone and other materials) and placed in the center of the room. In the tub bobbed bottles of special water, magnetized by Mesmer, although unclear exactly how. From out of the covered *baquet* radiated bent iron rods, intended to conduct the invisible magnetic fluid.

Patients stood around the tub in a circle, either holding hands to form a kind of magnetic ring or bound together with a light rope. After the candles were dimmed and soft music was put on in the background, some patients began to sweat or cry or laugh hysterically. If assistants noticed patients who weren't affected, they approached them and pressed their rods against their bodies.

Then, like a kind of Svengali, Mesmer entered, clothed in a lavender robe embroidered with flowers. He wandered from patient to patient, touching some with his wand and staring intently at others. As he did so, slowly, surely, a frenzy set in. A scientific commission later described its remarkable effects:

> Some of [the patients] are calm, tranquil and unconscious of any sensation; others cough, spit, are affected with a slight degree of pain, a partial or universal burning and perspiration; a third class are agitated and tormented with convulsions.

> The convulsions are rendered extraordinary by their frequency, their violence and their duration…they are characterized by involuntary jerking movements in all the limbs, and in the whole body, by contraction of the

throat, by twitchings in the hypochondriac
and epigastric regions, by dimness and rolling
of the eyes, by piercing cries, tears, hiccups
and immoderate laughter.

Mesmer considered this frenetic moment, which he
called the "magnetic crisis," the key stage in the healing
process; without it, a cure was impossible. So draining was
the process that many patients fainted or fell asleep afterward, later claiming they were cured.

Luminaries in politics and letters soon became either
patients or admirers of "the great enchanter." With new
confidence, Mesmer once again sought scientific approval.
But in Paris, as in Vienna, the public was much more wel-
coming than the academy. Mesmer found only one convert on Paris' Faculty of Medicine, Charles Deslon, an
attractive and influential member of the faculty.

Claiming he had been cured of stomach pains by animal magnetism, Deslon was an eager supporter—at least
at first. After Mesmer put together a somewhat muddled
list of 27 propositions of animal magnetism, Deslon presented them to a panel of his colleagues and proposed a
controlled experiment as a test. Not only did the faculty
turn its nose up at the proposal, it threatened to cut
Deslon loose unless he desisted from such unorthodox
rubbish. He persisted and then quit in 1780.

Mesmer was outraged and threatened to leave Paris.
Supporters rushed forward to dissuade him. In 1781 a
government minister acting on behalf of the queen
offered him 20,000 livres (francs) a year, as well as a
chateau for his *clinique*, if he would reveal his "secrets" to

three aspiring mesmerists named by the state. The increasingly suspicious Mesmer politely turned down the offer, convinced it was a ruse.

Within two years he was earning almost 350,000 livres a year from his own pupils. His instruction was offered under two conditions: that his students never reveal the secret of the treatment and that they offer half of their earnings to him. Because his students were wealthy members of the aristocracy, they didn't seem to mind. Soon, some of the hundred or so members of the "Society of Harmony" broke with Mesmer and went off in their own directions. One of them, the Marquis de Puységur, explored the potency of will power in animal magnetism, and later discovered somnambulism or sleepwalking.

Eventually the king began to worry about the influential and arrogant magnetizer. In 1784, at the request of Deslon, who had parted ways with Mesmer but had since set up a successful magnetist *clinique* of his own, the French government charged the Faculty of Medicine and the Royal Society of Medicine to investigate Mesmer and his fashionable cure. The commission from the Faculty of Medicine included Benjamin Franklin, then the American Ambassador to France and universally respected for his scientific acumen; Antoine Lavoisier, who discovered oxygen and had just co-published an important work on the nature of heat; and the astronomer Jean Sylvain Bailly. Even Joseph Guillotin was involved; his curious invention, the guillotine, would soon change the course of European history.

Mesmer was not invited to participate in the study; it was thought that Deslon's methods would be indicative of his teacher's. Deslon was confident that animal magnetism would finally be legitimized as a therapeutic practice. The inquiry, it should be noted, was designed to study *only* the mysterious curative agent behind animal magnetism. It was a tall order back then, and today it would be no less challenging. The force they sought was invisible, and the commission had to be careful not to upset the wealthy and powerful people who were supporters of the miraculous cure. After all, if Mesmer's success has proven anything, it was that scientific objectivity was often colored by societal mores.

The commissioners observed the effects of the *baquet* in Deslon's clinic. As if on cue, patients entered into the accustomed crises, even though an electrometer determined that the *baquet* contained no mineral magnetism or electric charge. Then members of the commission themselves, all in fine health, underwent treatment. The procedure produced absolutely no effects, making the commissioners wonder at the massive divide between animal magnetism's remarkable impact on the public and its negligible effects on them. Finally, sick members of the lower classes were singled out for testing. Only 5 of 14 showed any results.

One of the more creative tests of the magnetic fluid was conducted in Franklin's orchard. After Deslon magnetized a single apricot tree, a 12-year-old sick boy was led blindfolded into the orchard and told to embrace certain trees for two minutes each. At the first tree, he began to sweat, cough and complain of headaches. The symptoms worsened as he embraced other trees and eventually the boy fainted. The irony was that he had not come within 24 feet of the magnetized tree and had shown worsening symptoms at trees up to 38 feet away!

Ultimately, the commission from the Faculty of Medicine concluded that there was no evidence of a magnetic fluid, so the mysterious "crises" must be the result of a combination of "the touches of the operator, the excited imagination of the patient and the involuntary instinct of imitation." After commenting on the danger of the treatment, the faculty added that "all public treatment by Magnetism must in the long run have deplorable consequences."

A second report from the Royal Society of Medicine presented similar findings, with one important exception. One commissioner named de Jussieu was thoroughly impressed with what he had observed and affirmed the existence of a magnetic fluid called "animal heat," which he claimed eluded observation by scientific means. More importantly, he submitted that animal heat could be directed by the will of the magnetizer himself.

Such a conclusion was greatly at odds with Mesmer's own writings. To his dying day, he believed in the existence and power of the magnetic fluid and did not consider himself anything but a humble conduit. For more than 100 years, his followers grappled with the nature of the mysterious mesmeric power, creating a bizarre array of explanations and variations on animal magnetism. Those who were convinced it had psychological, not physical, origins share a bias with today's traveling hypnotist-charlatans, who promote the idea of the "strong-willed" hypnotist against the "weak-willed" subject.

As for Mesmer, the reports of the two commissions exacted a great toll. The Paris newspapers were unkind to his treatment, and soon burlesques were staged with mesmerism as their target. Meanwhile, members of the medical establishment emerged with stories of failed cures and relapses. There were some defenders among Mesmer's former students, but they could only stem the tide so much.

One unofficial report of the commissioners, intended only for the eyes of the king, even commented on the gender imbalance in animal magnetism, which invariably involved men magnetizing society women, many of whom were not the slightest bit ill. The implication was undeniable: animal magnetism made suggestible women swoon, almost in a kind of sexual frenzy, and was thus a risk to public morality.

With talk of a ban in the air, Mesmer started to quarrel with the Paris Society of Harmony. His desire to keep his secrets secret and retain a kind of exclusive control over mesmerism eventually led him to fall out with some of its members. The arrival of the great charlatan Cagliostro in Paris in 1785 distracted attention from Mesmer, but also moved him into the same camp of charlatans who preyed on the gullible. It's a shame because Mesmer was a doctor, not a confidence trickster—the idea of fraud would have been averse to him.

He departed Paris hastily, as he had Austria before, leaving all his belongings behind. During the French Revolution he traveled through Germany and Switzerland, eventually returning to Vienna. He was kept under police surveillance because the Austrian authorities suspected his affiliations with secret societies made him a dangerous reactionary. Many governments at the time feared even the slightest revolutionary agitators. In 1794, Mesmer was asked to leave and ended up working for 20 years as a country doctor in a small town near Zürich, Switzerland, until his death in 1815.

Mesmer made one final trip to France, to make a claim on what he had left behind before the revolution. The government granted him a fair-sized pension—no fortune, to be sure, but enough to live on. During his stay in Paris, Mesmer wrote a book, never translated into English, which revealed his interest in paranormal questions. In it, he made it clear that telepathy, precognition and clairvoyance were all facts to be explained by mechanical means. He felt that animal magnetism, which severed subjects' connections with the outer world and put them in touch with a kind of inner sense, could lead the way.

The disappointment, of course, was that Mesmer never provided a satisfactory explanation for this inner sense or why it only became apparent in the sick. It's almost as if he eagerly recognized the existence of the mysterious forces in question, but he could not understand them. Today we know the results he achieved with his *baquet* can be attributed to hysteria, repression, auto-suggestion and other psychological mechanisms. His idea that illness was not natural or physical, that it was based in a kind of mental stagnation, was picked up by his many followers, who went on to explore sleepwalking, hypnosis and even psychoanalysis.

Jeane Dixon
DON'T BOARD THAT PLANE

Jeane Dixon, known to some as the "Capitol Soothsayer," died in 1997 at age 79. Her accomplishments were impressive: seven books with three million copies sold, a beloved syndicated horoscope column and the adoration of many prominent politicians in her home of Washington, D.C. Perhaps such success is not accidental for someone who could foretell the future.

Dixon made many forecasts during her life, especially about political events, but much of her reputation rests on one sensational prediction: the assassination of President John F. Kennedy. The seeress was first alerted to the event in 1952. It is described in Ruth Montgomery's *A Gift of Prophecy*, a popular account of Dixon's life and gifts.

Dixon was meditating in St. Matthew's Cathedral in Washington one morning. As the rain fell outside, she felt a familiar yet unsettling sensation of withdrawal, a feeling that she often experienced before an important vision.

As she knelt down to pray, she saw a radiant vision of the White House. The numbers "1960" appeared above it. Then, she said, the numbers dissolved into a dark cloud and "dripped down like chocolate frosting on a chocolate cake." In front of the building stood a young, blue-eyed man with a shock of thick, brown hair. A voice told Dixon that he was a Democrat and would die violently while in office. Although the vision vanished suddenly, Dixon remained in a hazy state for several days.

Was Jeane Dixon truly able to predict the future?

The prediction was reported later in *Parade* magazine on May 13, 1956:

> Mrs. Dixon thinks [the 1960 presidential election] will be dominated by labor and won by a Democrat. He will be assassinated or die in office, "though not necessarily in his first term."

This Democrat turned out to be John F. Kennedy, who was still a Massachusetts senator when the prediction was published. In 1963, Dixon tried to warn the president not to travel to Dallas, where he was assassinated on November 22, but failed. She also predicted the death of Dag Hammerskjöld, the UN diplomat who perished in an airplane crash in Africa in September 1961.

Other predictions, less grim, revolved around political events. Three years before the Long March of Mao Zedong, Dixon predicted the establishment of communism in China; she also foresaw the Soviets launching a satellite into space four years before Sputnik.

Dixon's most remarkable non-political prediction involved Carole Lombard, a famous motion picture actress in the 1930s. At the time, Lombard was at the height of her career, having finished some of her best work in Ernest Lubitsch's *To Be or Not to Be*. In January 1942, after touching Lombard's hand, Dixon experienced a premonition of the actress' death. She warned her not to board any airplanes for the next six weeks. The patriotic movie star, who was involved in a government-sponsored tour to sell war bonds at the time, was unconvinced.

Lombard boarded a plane for Indianapolis three days after Dixon's warning. Nothing happened during the flight. Following the fundraiser, the actress decided to fly back to Hollywood instead of going by train as originally planned. Rumor had it that she was eager to speak her husband, Clark Gable, who was about to start filming a picture with the flirtatious Lana Turner. They had quarreled before she left.

Lombard never made it home. Her plane, redirected at the last minute to Las Vegas instead of Boulder, crashed shortly after take-off into Table Rock Mountain. The 33-year-old starlet was killed instantly. The crash site was one of the most fiery and mangled in U.S. aviation history.

. . .

Jeane Dixon was born on January 3, 1918, in Medford, Wisconsin, but grew up in California. When she was eight, her mother took her to a gypsy fortune-teller, who predicted that the little girl would become a psychic and advise powerful leaders.

In 1939, Jeane married James L. Dixon, a California auto dealer; the pair later moved to Washington, D.C., where James worked as a real estate executive. Jeane served as his assistant for many years while giving psychic readings to servicemen and government workers during World War II. Her reputation grew to such an extent that, she claimed, she was invited to the White House during Franklin D. Roosevelt's fourth (and final) term to offer a "reading." She correctly predicted then that he had only a few months to live.

Later, during the Reagan administration, Dixon advised Nancy Reagan, who was well known for her interest in astrology. Though the First Lady later fell out with Dixon, choosing to rely on rival astrologer Joan Quigley, the association speaks to her influence in Washington. Strom Thurmond, the outspoken Republican senator from South Carolina, even asked Dixon to be a godmother to one of his children.

In spite of her reputation, Dixon wasn't perfect. Some predictions, such as the fall of the Berlin Wall and Russia's becoming an ally of the U.S., did not happen in the time frames she set forth. Others, such as her revelation that World War III would begin in 1958 in a dispute over two offshore Chinese islands, were simply wrong.

Dixon even made some forecasts in which the *reverse* proved to be true. She was convinced, for instance, that the Vietnam conflict would be over by 1966. In fact, that year saw the heaviest air raids of the war and an escalation in troop deployments, leading to massive demonstrations the next year. Dixon also predicted that the Soviets would be first to land on the moon. In 1978, the year after Dixon thought super-intelligent humans would to arrive from outer space, she claimed that Pope Paul VI would "surprise the world with his energy and determination." Shortly thereafter the pontiff fell ill and died!

Critics, of course, were highly suspicious of Dixon. John Allen Paulos, an academic who wrote several popular books about the public ignorance of mathematics, even coined the phrase "the Jeane Dixon effect." He was convinced that people, and especially journalists, tend to focus on correct predictions and overlook false ones. In a letter to James Randi, a fellow skeptic, the science fiction and fantasy writer L. Sprague de Camp coined another relevant term, "credophile," who

> ...gets positive pleasure from belief and pain from doubt...The credophile collects beliefs the way a jackdaw does nest ornaments: not for utility but for glitter. And, once having embraced a belief, it takes something more than mere disproof to make him let go.

If credophiles are quick to offer loose interpretations of predictions, critics can just as easily "prove" that some of Dixon's predictions are entirely the opposite. Take one of the psychic's most famous—and as yet unfulfilled—predictions:

> A child who was born in the Middle East on the fifth of February 1962, will revolutionize the world, and in due time unite all conflicting faiths and denominations into one all encompassing faith.

This person, the subject of some of Dixon's clearest visions, would be born into a family of poor farmers. Dixon added that humanity will know the enormous strength of this man about the year of 1980, and his power will grow until 1999, when there will be "peace on earth for all men of good will."

Some might argue that the opposite is the case. Osama bin Laden, undoubtedly one of the most famous men in the world, was born into a wealthy Saudi Arabian family in 1957. Osama's father, however, was a poor laborer until he managed to build a powerful construction dynasty. Around 1980 bin Laden began operations in Afghanistan; what he learned there would lead ultimately to his involvement with the terrorists who engineered the terrible attacks on America in 2001. Instead of uniting the peoples of the world in goodwill, bin Laden helped to embroil the world in greater conflict.

This small example shows that data in prophecies can be bent to fit desired conclusions, as is often the case with predictions made by the astrologer Nostradamus.

The subject of Dixon's predictions is also worth noting. Predicting political events such as elections or races to the moon, in which only two or three outcomes are possible, is more straightforward than, say, predicting which of the 32 NFL teams will win the Super Bowl (although we can be certain it won't be the Jets or the Lions).

Moreover, a psychic with a keen knowledge of international politics, as Dixon had, would be more likely to make accurate predictions than, say, someone with zero political knowledge who might possess equally powerful psychic abilities. Which begs the question: why were Dixon's abilities restricted to mostly political figures and events, i.e., figures in the public spotlight? Isn't it possible that psychics, whose powers are difficult to harness, would have visions about mundane events and persons?

Whatever the case, there's no denying the public support for Jeane Dixon. Some people adored her for reasons that had nothing to do with her powers per se. Along with being a devout Catholic who was convinced her gift came from God, Dixon never charged anyone for a psychic consultation or sought to profit from her gifts. Whatever profits accrued from her column or books she placed in a charitable children's foundation that she started in 1964. Perhaps the memory of her kind face and generosity will survive long after her prophecies are forgotten.

5
Charlatans Galore

Miss Cleo
THE PSYCHIC HOTLINE

It was 3:39 AM. You couldn't sleep, you'd been tossing for hours. All your bills were due the next day. You dragged yourself to the TV, security blanket in tow, to see if maybe, just maybe, a *Golden Girls* rerun was on. Half the channels had Ron Popeil and miracle cures, the other half those color bars and the "beeeeep" tone. But one channel, with a captivating Jamaican psychic, seemed to invite you in.

It was Miss Cleo, the face of her eponymous "psychic hotline." Clad in a turban and fingering a deck of tarot cards, she urged you to call her for a *free* three-minute tarot-card reading. *Free?* You groggily caved in and dialed the 1-800 number. Only you didn't talk to Cleo herself; as a "preferred customer," you were passed along to one of her "psychic associates" at a different number.

The operator spent several minutes taking down your personal information, then she passed you off to another operator. This woman offered a reading, occasionally making an accurate, if vague, observation about your personal life. You hung up after 20 minutes, somewhat satisfied. But when the bill arrived a few weeks later, the "free" reading had turned into a $100 tab. But that was only the beginning…

Similar scenarios were played out countless times from 1999 to 2002, when Miss Cleo's Psychic Hotline was offering advice on love, money and family to insomniacs everywhere.

It was nothing new. Telephone psychics emerged in the early 1990s when TV direct marketing combined with

Miss Cleo, a.k.a. Youree Dell Harris, fleeced millions of American insomniacs as a TV tarot card reader.

high-tech call centers. Programs such as the Psychic Friends Network, with celebrity endorser Dionne Warwick, started to pop up during cheap, late-night ad slots. They offered telephone readings from psychics, at inflated rates, for callers over 18 years of age.

Miss Cleo's program was run by the Psychic Readers Network (PRN) and Access Resource Services (ARS). Their owners, Florida businessmen Steven Feder and Peter Stolz, are purportedly the biggest operators in the psychic audiotext industry. From Miss Cleo's operation alone their companies collected $500 million and billed consumers for twice that figure. The pair hired Miss Cleo to act as the spokesperson for their hotline.

But like many who profit from psychic readings, Feder and Stolz got greedy and starting bending the rules. In February 2002, after more than 2000 complaints of false advertising, crooked billing tactics and telemarketing harassment, the U.S. Federal Trade Commission filed a lawsuit in Florida against PRN and ARS. Later the same year, the companies agreed to go off the air, cancel $500 million in customer service bills and return all uncashed cheques. They also agreed to pay the government a $5 million fine.

Although ARS never admitted to wrongdoing during the settlement, claiming its practices were within the law, it deliberately misled millions of callers by promising free readings or misrepresenting to callers the nature of long-distance charges.

ARS's collection agencies repeatedly called and harassed consumers and others, often ignoring requests that persistent calls stop. Mail was sent out in misleading official-looking envelopes: "U.S. Mail ... Important Confidential Document ... Buy And Hold U.S. Savings Bonds." Assuming that it was a government document, people who received the mail felt obligated to pay or call, worried their credit would be affected. But because the service was misleadingly advertised, often no such obligation existed.

One woman from Cheektowaga, New York, who never called the hotline, made the following complaint on consumeraffairs.com:

> One of my friends decided to try the Cleo Psychic Network to see what his free reading would be. After being on hold to speak to a psychic for over 3 minutes, he felt it wasn't worth it and hung up. Ever since then we've been receiving *numerous* phone calls from 1-000-000-0000 (as seen on our Caller-ID).

Every time I requested someone say hello, there was no answer.

Today, after the third time of this number showing up, a person finally cleared his voice before speaking and said he wanted to speak to the head of the household. Concerned about how this person got our phone number, I asked how he got it (seeing as it's unlisted). He avoided the question several times and kept saying he was from ARI and that I had to write down this very important phone number for an *urgent* message for the head of the household. He was very adamant about it and wouldn't even let me speak to his supervisor to get our phone number off the database.

I reluctantly called the *free* 1-800 number then was told it was from Cleo and that I had to call this 1-900 number for a free psychic reading up to 5 minutes. Desperate to contact *someone* to get us off this *stupid aggravating list*, I called the 1-900 number being very careful not to go over the 5 minutes. I finally got switched to a psychic (who didn't even know my name—what a good psychic!) and asked that our phone number be removed from whatever database they have. She said that because she is only a psychic, she couldn't do it. I asked for a number I could call to get removed—she didn't have one.

Needless to say, many people were relieved when the service shut down.

What of Miss Cleo? She wasn't, as her billing implied, a "Nationally Acclaimed Master Tarot Reader and Psychic." Nor was she Jamaican. According to records obtained by the Florida attorney general, Youree Dell Harris was born in Los Angeles on August 12, 1962, to parents from Texas and California. During a deposition in a Florida court in June 2002, the elusive Harris repeatedly invoked her Fifth Amendment right against self-incrimination when questioned about her birth documents.

D. Parvaz, a reporter for the *Seattle Post-Intelligencer*, discovered the likely source Harris' on-screen persona. From 1996 to 1997, Harris, a drifter then known as Ree Perris, was a playwright and actor. She was given money by the Langston Hughes Cultural Arts Center in Seattle, a non-profit organization, to produce three of her plays. In *For Women Only*, Perris portrayed a Jamaican woman named Cleo—presumably the prototype for Miss Cleo.

Interviews with cast members on Perris' productions revealed that several were never paid for their work. They stated that Perris, who falsely claimed to be a graduate of USC's theater arts program, had promised to pay them after she covered costly medical bills for cancer. Then she skipped town, eventually finding steady work as Miss Cleo. Today she resides in South Florida, probably living off the money she made as America's most infamous TV psychic.

If Miss Cleo was a phony, so were the thousands of "psychic associates" who stood by awaiting your call. According to Jim Gaines, who wrote an exposé of Cleo's hotline in the *New Times Broward-Palm Beach* (Florida) in 2002, the associates were recruited and trained by communications subcontractors, such as Buckwood Industries of Nevada or the Florida-based Real Communications Services, to use readings and other means to keep callers on the line for as long as possible. One operator even admitted to a Court TV reporter that an effective technique was to imply that a caller's spouse had been unfaithful. This tactic inevitably led to a string of worried questions—and higher phone bills.

Operators who consistently failed to keep callers on the line for 20 minutes or more, racking up bills in excess of $100, were at risk of losing their jobs. A priority system, meanwhile, favored the psychic associates who could keep callers calling.

The "readings" they offered were often scripted; operators had cue cards in front of them with instructions on how to proceed, including notes such as "BECOME MORE SINCERE NOW." The material wasn't original. In July 2001, a tarot expert named Nancy Garen, author of the popular guide *Tarot Made Easy* (1989), learned that phone readings and material from Miss Cleo's web site were being cribbed directly from her book. Garen succeeded in getting an injunction preventing ARS from using her material.

What did the Miss Cleo scam reveal? For one, *caveat emptor*—let the buyer beware. Unlike, say, the sprockets industry, where consumers buy a product at a certain price, aware of what they're getting, psychics often peddle a murky, intangible product—advice about people's personal lives. That is why "FOR ENTERTAINMENT ONLY" always appeared at the bottom of the screen when Miss Cleo was on. Such an innocuous disclaimer protected ARS from fraud by implying that the product for sale was not truthful or based on expert knowledge, but a simple, although expensive, way to pass the time.

José Arigó
THE PSYCHIC SURGEON?

A small city north of Rio de Janiero, Brazil, 1954. Fifteen people wait in a crammed kitchen adjacent to a makeshift operating room. The room is silent, except for the coughing of a sick baby being rocked by her mother. She and the others appear troubled and hopeful; they look almost as they might look before entering confession. At the slightest sound from the next room, all heads turn toward the rickety wooden door. Around the handle there are faint traces of a dark liquid, probably blood.

Suddenly a plump, muscular man with a moustache enters. He is not dressed as a doctor, but he shows the same self-assuredness and even impatience. Wiping his hand on his shirt, he asks for the next patient.

A woman, clearly the next in line, rises reverently.

"Doctor, my Tomás is very ill," she says in a rural accent, helping a young but obese man to his feet. "He has a lump under his rib. We have only this ring for payment."

"No money. Bring him."

They enter a dingy room with a twin bed in the middle. It looks like a surgery theater from the 19th century, without the anesthesia or the sense of scientific gravity. In the corner, a faucet drips into a drain in the floor.

Tomás lays on the bed and the surgeon lifts his shirt. With heavy, confident hands he kneads the boy's flabby abdomen. Then he picks up an old pocket knife. Surely, quickly, he makes a sudden slashing move that appears to be rough cutting. A small amount of blood oozes from the cut. He reaches into the cut and appears to extract an ugly red mass, probably a tumor. The mother looks away. He drops the bloody mess in a plastic pail. After massaging the skin, he releases his hand. The skin flexes back into shape and the incision, apart from a small nick, is gone. It is over in less than two minutes.

"Done. Say a prayer to the almighty."

The mother presses her hands together as if to pray; joyful tears stream down her cheek. Her son still lays flat, with his eyes shut tightly, anticipating pain. The surgeon rests his hand on the patient's shoulder and smiles. Tomás slowly open his eyes and looks down at his abdomen. He realizes the reports are all true. He is healed!

Or is he?

This fictional account is based on what is known of José Arigó, a famous "psychic surgeon." During the heyday of "psychic surgery" in the 1960s and 1970s, Arigó and other charlatans in the Phillipines and Brazil used techniques reminiscent of stage magic to "cure" people with serious ailments. The phenomenon deserves discussion as one of the greatest paranormal scams ever.

Psychic surgery involves opening and closing the body either without surgical instruments or with crude instruments. Practices varied, although the procedures were always conducted under septic conditions without anesthetic. Some surgeons claimed that they were not operating on the physical body as much as on the "perispirit" or ethereal body of the patient. Their healing powers consisted in merely passing their hands over the affected areas. Others such as Arigó used pocket knives or even fingers to penetrate the skin and remove lumpy, bloody tumors. Patients were sealed up without stitches and walked away unscathed.

Nothing from Arigó's background hinted at his eventual fame. Born José Pedro de Freitas in Congonhas do Campo, Brazil, in 1918, he was a peasant with a third-grade education. He worked on his father's farm and as a miner before running a restaurant with his father's money. The name "Arigó," which means something like "good-natured but not very bright" in Portuguese, was given to him by his friends. He was deeply involved in local politics, narrowly losing a small-town mayoral election in 1954.

His first breakthrough came while a chronically ill relative lay on her deathbed, receiving her last rites. Suddenly possessed, Arigó rushed to the kitchen, grabbed a knife and plunged it into the woman. He then reached inside her and pulled out an enormous tumor, which he dropped into a nearby sink with the knife. Doctors summoned to the scene determined that the woman had been cured without hemorrhaging or pain.

As word of Arigó's gift spread, people flocked to Congonhas do Campo to be cured.

By the time of his death, the grassroots miracle worker claimed to have healed as many as 500,000 patients and had been the focus of many stories in the media. It seems even more remarkable when you consider that he kept another full-time job and did not charge for his work.

During operations, Arigó claimed to fall into trances, sometimes speaking in German or with a German accent. His spirit control was one Dr. Adolphus Fritz, a German medical student who apparently lived in the 1800s. According to Arigó, Dr. Fritz was born in Munich, practiced in Poland and died in Estonia early in the 20th century. After Arigó became famous, many people tried to confirm the doctor's identity, but no evidence of his existence has ever been uncovered. Arigó also identified two other controls under Dr. Fritz's direction: "Gilbert Pierre," a French ophthalmologist; and "Takahaski," a Japanese specialist in tumor removal.

Arigó preferred to use his trademark instrument, a rusty pocket knife, although he often operated with other blades, sometimes even with the dull side. On several occasions he was seen using his bare hands. Extremely nimble, he was capable of treating up to 60 patients in as many minutes and rarely required more than 90 seconds for even the most complicated procedures. And while he never used disinfectant, observers claimed that Arigó's patients never suffered post-operative infections.

As a "doctor," Arigó also wrote prescriptions, which were nearly as important as his miraculous surgeries. But because his handwriting was nearly illegible, only a man named Altimiro, his handy assistant, could interpret them. The medicines were often outdated and prescribed in dangerous doses.

Inevitably, curiosity seekers soon arrived on the scene. In 1968, Dr. Andrija Puharich, an American neurologist and parapsychologist who later handled publicity for Uri Geller, came to investigate. He brought some Americans with him, a small team consisting of photographers, physicians, a psychiatrist and two psychic healers.

Puharich had a benign lymphoma near his right elbow and volunteered to go under the knife. As a crew filmed the procedure, Arigó impulsively grabbed the real doctor's arm. Instructing his patient to look away, he quickly made an incision without anesthetic and removed the growth. It was all over in a matter of seconds, and the cut healed in three or four days without becoming infected. A shocked Puharich had no explanation, but he failed to take X-rays before and after the procedure to provide conclusive evidence.

The Brazilian Medical Association, however, eventually sued Arigó for illegal practice of medicine. In 1957 he was sentenced to 15 months in jail and forced to pay a sizable fine and court costs; an appeal reduced the prison term. But Arigó's supporters, including then-president of Brazil, Juscelino Kubitschek, who met Arigó while campaigning in 1955, rushed to his defense. Kubitschek's daughter was beset by kidney stones shortly after the election, so he approached Arigó, who wrote a prescription that apparently cured her. In gratitude, the president secured a pardon for the miracle worker.

Arigó ran afoul of the law again in 1964; he was charged with practicing medicine illegally and even witchcraft. Judge Filipe Immensi sentenced him to 16 months. Shortly after the trial, Dr. Puharich, who remained convinced of Arigó's remarkable abilities, approached Immensi. He convinced the judge to test them for himself.

Immensi witnessed the imprisoned Arigó remove a cataract from a woman's eye with a pair of scissors. He described it in his report:

> I saw him pick up a pair of nail scissors. He wiped them on his shirt and used no disinfectant. I saw him then cut straight into the cornea of the patient's eye. She did not flinch, although perfectly conscious. The cataract was out in seconds…Arigó said a prayer and a few drops of blood appeared on the cotton in his hand. He wiped the woman's eye with it and she was cured.

Immensi was impressed with the feat, but he couldn't bend the law. Arigó ended up serving 9 months instead of the original 16, although he was given permission to heal people while imprisoned. After his release, the healer continued to practice. He died in an automobile accident in 1971.

What's remarkable about Arigó—and what sets him apart from folk healers and shamans—is that a team of American doctors lead by Puharich legitimated his miraculous faith healing. But Puharich's own success story, as we have seen, was not beyond doubt. No evidence of his condition before and after ever surfaced, and Puharich's positive endorsement of another charlatan, Uri Geller, makes him an unreliable witness.

So how exactly did Arigó pull the wool over so many eyes? In his book *Mediums, Mystics and the Occult*, Milbourne Christopher, an accomplished stage magician, shows how one skeptic exposed the chicanery.

Joe Pyne, an irreverent California TV and radio personality in the 1970s, loved to expose frauds on his shows. After several positive reports about Dr. Tony Agpaoa, the most famous of the Philipino surgeons, Pyne traveled to Manila with a camera crew to oversee the so-called *curanderos* first hand. Upon his return, Pyne hired a man and woman to stage a psychic surgery on the air. Christopher offered this account.

> During the kneading of the abdomen, the left hand squeezed and formed a fold in the flesh. When the "cut" was made, the "surgeon" filled the cavity with red liquid from a sponge concealed in his right hand. The wiping away of the "blood" gave the surgeon the opportunity to palm a bit of animal tissue and force it into the cavity as he reached down "into the body" with his fingers. Then he dramatically pulled the gory mess from the "cut."

Throughout this maneuver his left fingers exerted pressure to maintain the illusion that an incision had been made in the flesh. Finally he covered the "cut" with the palm of his right hand and released the fold of skin which had been held by his left fingers. The flesh returned to its normal tautness before his right hand was lifted. Since there had been no incision, there was no scar.

In Arigó's procedures, in which a small cut was left behind, Christopher theorized that the surgeon could have made a very small nick in the skin with his makeshift scalpel. When the blood from this nick collected in the fold of skin, it appeared as a genuine incision. But as soon as the surgeon released the folded skin, after removing the "palmed" tumor, only the nick remained. And because it was very small, it stopped bleeding very quickly, giving the impression that the patient had been miraculously healed.

As for the miraculous cataract excisions, Arigó probably placed the blunt edge of a knife against the eye or slipped it under the eyelid, then moved it gently across the cornea. While this seems very dangerous, in the hands of someone as dextrous as Arigó it was just another part of the show.

It's no coincidence that psychic surgeons became popular in Third World countries, where people are desperately poor and uneducated. Here, miracle cures have the best chance of success, especially when the doctor is as convinced of the efficacy of the treatment as the patient. By performing an otherwise daunting medical procedure in a painless way, Arigó removed fear from surgery and secured the trust of hundreds of thousands. His success also highlights a very important factor in paranormal celebrity—the credulity of the media. Many tabloid-style stories ran in the Brazilian press on the healer, and they helped to transform anecdotal claims into hard facts.

Charles H. Foster
PELLET READING

A séance was being held in a room at the Exeter Hotel in Boston. Outside, a foghorn bellowed into the sunny harbor and horseshoes clicked across Beacon Hill's cobblestones.

"Ladies and gentlemen, before you are small pieces of paper," said Mr. Charles Foster of Salem, Massachusetts, gesturing expressively at a table with his right hand. "Use it or your own paper, it makes no difference. Please write down the names of your beloved dear departed, either family or friends, then roll the paper into pea-sized pellets and place them here. If you have written the names out beforehand, please, I implore you, wait until I am away to deposit them."

The medium took a moment to run his left hand over his shock of thick black hair, parted in the middle. Then he closed his eyes.

"I shall now leave the room," he continued. "Upon my return I will reveal the names to you in a truly incredible manner."

As Foster strolled toward the door, Mrs. Elizabeth Smith, on holiday from New Hampshire with her husband Robert, stared blankly at a painting on the wall. Foster's mention of the deceased called to mind her beloved son William, who had died of consumption three years ago. The prospect of Foster's contacting her son's spirit terrified and excited her. Although she hadn't told Robert, it was the reason why she convinced him to come in the first place.

The young couple beside them, the only others in attendance, appeared to have prepared their pellets in advance; clearly they were veterans of the burgeoning Spiritualism fad, not novices as she and her husband were. Not wanting to seem green, Eliza fetched the small slips of paper and gave a handful to Robert. Both wrote "Billy," William's nickname, as well as the names of other dead relations. Robert's sister Anna had recently died in during childbirth, and Maureen O'Hara, Eliza's grandmother, had succumbed to hay fever only days before her 60th birthday.

Robert was careful to cover his hand as he wrote. As a grammar school principal who paid careful attention to anti-Spiritualist sermons during mass, he was not taking any chances. He collected Eliza's pellets, which were no larger than grape seeds, and walked to the front of the room. After laying them on the elegant mahogany table, he mixed his pellets up very thoroughly with those of the other couples. Unbeknownst to his wife, Robert had left five or six of his pellets blank. He sat down and smiled.

Foster's heavy footsteps startled the group a minute later. He now appeared to be under the influence of some otherworldly force. In plain view he methodically ran his fingers over the pellets, moving them around the table but taking up none. Then he then began to push them towards the sitters, uttering names in a steady stream, until he stopped his strange incantation. "Billy Smith," he said after a brief pause. "The name of this person will appear on my arm."

Before the sitters could return quizzical looks, Foster rolled up his left sleeve, revealing his bare arm. There, in red letters that rose slightly above his pale skin, was the name "Billy Smith."

Eliza fainted in her chair. Even as Robert pulled her upright, his mouth hung open in astonishment. The other couple was frozen too. Surveying the scene, satisfied with his labors, Foster smiled.

• • •

This routine, combining "pellet reading" and "dermography," was the trademark of Foster, who became a very successful Spiritualist medium in the 1860s and 1870s. While he was hardly a household name—his fame pales beside that of D.D. Home or the Fox sisters—Foster remains an interesting anomaly of the early Spiritualist movement.

He was unlike other mediums of the day. He frequented loud bars and was hopelessly addicted to thick cigars. Yet his affections for flowers and fine music, as well as friendships in the world of opera and poetry, lent him an unusual air of civility. That he usually traveled in the company of an attractive male secretary may have caused some suspicions, although they did nothing to dim his appeal.

Foster's biographer, George C. Bartlett, offered the following description in *Salem Seer* (1891):

> He was extravagantly dual. He was not only Dr. Jekyll and Mr. Hyde, but he represented half a dozen different Jekylls and Hydes…He was an unbalanced genius, and at times I should say, insane…He wore out many of his friends. He seemed impervious to the opinions of others, and apparently yielded to every desire.

Perhaps his unusual family, who regularly encountered spirits, was partly to blame. Born in 1838 in Salem, Massachusetts, Foster was educated in public schools. Epes Sargent, a writer of some fame from nearby Gloucester, wrote that Foster's first paranormal moment came at 14, when he heard raps on his desk at school. At home, where his deceased aunt Bessie would appear now and then to rummage through her old belongings, the young medium was beset by poltergeists. By 24, he was a successful medium whose controls included famous literary celebrities such as Virgil, Cervantes and Camoens.

Foster invented pellet reading and it became his specialty. The other component of his routine, writing on skin or "dermography," was not his invention. That honor rested with a Mrs. Seymour of Waukegan, Illinois, whose spirit communications appeared on her bare arms. Seymour would write the message on her arm with the tip of her finger, then watch as letters materialized in bright red a few moments later. After 15 to 20 minutes, they vanished.

Foster toured England from 1861 to 1863. While there, he added materializations of hands and other objects to his retinue. Word quickly spread of Foster's exploits, and a number of literary celebrities, including Charles Dickens, William Thackeray and Alfred, Lord Tennyson, sat with him. During four séances at Newcastle-Upon-Tyne, Foster was expected to divine the names of the 40 sitters, whose names were kept in a notebook at a separate location. According to an objective observer, Foster had only a three percent margin of error.

Another event, witnessed by Dr. John Ashburner and described in his book *Philosophy of Animal Magnetism and Spiritualism* (1867), seems to indicate that Foster's dermography could occur involuntarily.

Ashburner, a prominent London physician, had invited Foster to his home on several occasions to conduct séances in front of society guests. At two o'clock in the morning one night, Foster's frantic roommate awoke the doctor, claiming the medium was dangerously ill. Ashburner rushed to his room and, upon examination, determined that Foster was extremely intoxicated after a long night of drinking. After prescribing a purgative, the doctor and the roommate looked down at Foster. In Ashburner's words,

> Suddenly the bedclothes were tightly rolled downwards as far as his groin. The shirt was then rolled tightly, like a cord, exposing to our view the skin of the chest and abdomen. Soon there appeared in large red letters raised on the surface the word 'DEVELOPMENT,' which extended from the right groin to the left shoulder, dividing the surface into two rectangular compartments. These were filled up with sprigs of flowers, resembling fleur-de-lys. The phenomenon lasted nearly ten minutes, when the shirt and the bedclothes were unrolled gently and replaced as they were at first.

Though remarkable, this incident hints at Foster's excessive lifestyle, which occasionally disagreed with British propriety. By 1863, the English had had their fill, especially after the editor of *Spiritual* magazine received a letter describing "sickening details of [Foster's] criminality in another direction that we should no longer soil our pages with his mediumship." Slater Brown, who wrote a captivating portrait of Foster in his book *The Heyday of Spiritualism*, was similarly oblique in describing his "hidden vices and undisclosed propensities." What these were we will never know. Foster left England for Paris to appear before Napoleon III, and later went to Australia before returning to New York.

As with many mediums, skeptics set out to expose Foster at every turn. In his book *The Bottom Facts Concerning the Science of Spiritualism* (1883), John Truesdell reports that Foster was caught in 1872 palming the pellets and reading them while relighting his cigar. An Englishman offered a more far-fetched explanation, arguing that Foster was able to decipher what was being written by watching the movements of the top end of the pencil. As evidence, he submitted that he had himself carefully concealed his hand and considered Foster's subsequent inability to identify the name he wrote a failure. This theory seems unlikely, especially since Foster often detected the names on pellets that had been scribbled out in advance. As for his skin writing, skeptics advanced that to achieve the effect Foster would scratch his arm with a dull pencil, making red marks that disappeared after several minutes. This was never proved.

One skeptic, George A. Syme, the owner and editor of a newspaper in Melbourne, Australia, tried unsuccessfully to trip up Foster while he was on tour. Syme had a friend named Scrutator bring a book to one of Foster's séances. It was tightly wrapped in opaque paper and Scrutator knew nothing of its contents. After Foster's routine, Scrutator approached him and asked him to identify the title of the book and the author's name. Foster wrote the word "politics" on a sheet of paper. Scrutator, expecting greater detail, was unimpressed and told Foster as much. Foster replied that the spirits he was in contact with could not see the book.

Now convinced that Foster had failed, Scrutator unwrapped the small volume. The book, a collection of articles from the London *Daily News*, was entitled *Political Portraits*. Because there was no single author, Foster felt vindicated that he had not identified one. As further evidence of his powers, he placed his hand on the book, then said he would ask the spirits to offer a word or two from the text. In short order a message was rapped out: "Turn to page 120, top of the page—'Masters say.'" In an article Syme wrote for his newspaper, he explained that the medium opened book to the appropriate page. The pages were new and uncut, so he carefully tore them open. Sure enough, the first words on the page read "Masters say."

This episode resists an easy explanation. But like many paranormal celebrities, Foster's powers wavered. One day, supporters were baffled by him, the next day skeptics cried foul. His character was equally changeable, swerving from giddy to grumpy with little warning. Foster seems to have self-medicated with the drink, and it eventually caught up with him.

In 1881 he was admitted to Danvers Insane Asylum. According to newspaper reports, he was diagnosed as an alcoholic who suffered from a softening of the brain, although he more likely suffered from a psychological disorder. During his final years, an aunt apparently took care of him. He was far gone by this time, prone to staring into space for hours on end. He died in 1888.

Henry Slade
RISE AND FALL

"Slate writing," a séance room sensation during the heyday of Spiritualism, was a form of "autography" or spirit writing. The medium and the sitter took positions at the opposite ends of a small table. Each grasped the corner of an ordinary school slate—a kind of mini-chalkboard—pressing it firmly against the underside of the table, with the writing side against the wood. A small piece of writing pencil was placed upon the slate to allow the spirit something to write with. Following the typical séance room invocations, light scratching sounds were heard, apparently the work of the spirit, followed by raps or another sign to indicate that message was finished. When the slates were placed upon the table, writing was evident. The text was either a message from the world of the spirits or an answer to a question previously scribbled down by the sitter.

The American-born medium Henry Slade did not invent slate writing, but he popularized it and was probably responsible for its decline. His initial successes, even under scientific scrutiny, were so great that a number of skeptics set out to expose him. His shifting fortunes reflect the sensationalistic nature of Spiritualism, in which mediums rose and fell like bowling pins, as well as the growing chasm between skeptics and believers, which persists to this day.

Slade's personal life is cloaked in mystery. Apart from estimates of his birth year, 1825, and place, Albion, Michigan, nothing is known of his parents, upbringing or education. His title of "doctor" was unsupported by any credential. All his contemporaries had to go on, apart from his skill with spirit controls and the slate, was his appearance and lively manner. Tall, handsome and slender, he wore elegant suits and classy diamond rings. During séances, audiences were mesmerized by his captivating eyes and his façade of utter sincerity—a quality shared by other top Spiritualist mediums.

Slade's slate-reading became a sensation after he arrived in London, en route to Russia, in July 1876. He gave many sittings and welcomed examinations from believers and skeptics alike. Slade's spirit controls rapped on tables, made objects levitate and coaxed accordions to play on their own. They also levitated chairs in full light and pinched sitters with unseen fingers in semi-dark séance rooms. Slade made such an impression that one journalist, writing in *The Spiritual Magazine*, declared the neophyte a fitting replacement for Daniel Dunglas Home, the most famous physical medium of all time.

Men of science such as Lord Raleigh and Frank Podmore, both skeptics with respect to the paranormal, watched Slade's séances and walked away dumbfounded. Others, however, were not so willing to abandon their doubts.

Early in September 1876, a zoologist called Sir Edmund Ray Lancaster decided to do everything in his power to expose Slade's chicanery. Lancaster considered it revenge for being outvoted during a committee meeting at the British Association for the Advancement of Science in which the board accepted a paper from another member who was sympathetic to Spiritualism. Convinced such superstitious hocus-pocus had gone too far, Lancaster attended a Slade séance with his friend Dr. Donkin. They each paid £1 and waited.

During the second sitting, before the scratching began and before Slade had time to react, Lancaster ripped the slate from the medium's hand, revealing a message already inscribed. Lancaster took this prepared message as an indisputable proof of trickery. On September 16, he published the exposure in the *London Times* and sued Slade for collecting money under false pretenses.

Apart from placing Slade's career in jeopardy, the case spurred a bitter feud between skeptics and believers. Some believed that Lancaster had unfairly interrupted a paranormal phenomenon at work, while others felt vindicated that the medium's secret had finally been discovered. Podmore described Slade's response to the scandal:

> The Spiritualists were perhaps justified in not accepting the incident as conclusive. Slade defended himself by asserting that, immediately before the slate was snatched from his hand, he heard the spirit writing, and had said so, but that his words were lost in the confusion which followed.

The trial began on October 1, 1876, at the Bow Street Police Court in London. Only four witnesses were allowed to testify in Slade's defense. The magistrate dismissed their testimony, insisting that his decision be based on "inferences to be drawn from the known course of nature." On the basis of Lancaster's deposition, he sentenced Slade to imprisonment and three months of hard labor.

The conviction was overturned on a technicality, but before the court could issue a second summons, Slade fled the country. He contacted Lancaster from Prague, offering himself up for testing. Lancaster made no reply, and Slade did not return to London until 1888 and then only under the assumed name of "Dr. Wilson." Thus began Slade's long and ultimately fruitless quest to re-establish his credibility.

Slade wandered Europe, traveling to Berlin, The Hague and Denmark, seeking approval from experts. He arrived in Leipzig, Germany, in December 1877 and offered to participate in experiments by Johann Zöllner, a well-known scientist. While it sounded complicated, the idea behind Zöllner's "fourth dimension" theory was simple enough: if spirit mediums occupied another dimension, just as real as the third dimension of ordinary experience, they should have the power to move objects from their dimension to ours. Simple experiments would prove or disprove this hypothesis.

Slade succeeded in some tests. Besides demonstrating slate writing under controlled conditions, he was able to put rings on wooden legs, tie knots in pieces of endless string and remove coins from sealed boxes. It's conceivable that he pulled these off using basic skills as a conjurer. But in more daunting tests, which did not permit deception, Slade was stumped. He could not place a candle inside a sealed bulb, nor could he link two rings made of different kinds of wood. If he was indeed in contact with controls in the fourth dimension, these tasks would have presented no obstacles: his mediums could have carried out the necessary manipulation in their dimension, then returned the objects in question to ours.

In spite of the mixed results, Slade considered the results a great success. He was perhaps supported by Zöllner, who published a favorable account of him in a book, which appeared in translation under the title *Transcendental Physics* (1878). Slade then traveled to Paris and befriended Camille Flammarion, a famous science writer and astronomer. Flammarion proposed another test. He sealed two slates together so that if Slade tampered with them he could not escape detection. A small piece of slate pencil was placed between the slates. Slade accepted the conditions of the experiment. The two adjourned to his apartment, where Slade's séance lasted no less than 10 days. When Flammarion examined the slates after the marathon session, there was not the slightest trace of writing inside.

Undaunted, Slade continued his wanderings, first to Russia, then briefly to England before setting off for Australia. After a long absence from America, Slade settled permanently in New York in 1885. The same year, he made an unfortunate miscalculation by appearing before the Seybert Commission in Philadelphia.

The commission, set up by Spiritualist Henry Seybert with funding from the University of Pennsylvania, caught the medium red-handed on several occasions. Slade was seen surreptitiously removing his foot from a slipper and using his toes to touch nearby sitters. On another occasion, before a session of slate writing, one of his "blank" slates was shown to have writing on it.

Among other things, the commission established a key difference between writing on the medium's slates. For general messages, the writing was legible with appropriate punctuation. But on slates that offered replies to questions put by sitters, the writing was scarcely legible and vague, sometimes barely making sense. The commission ventured that the general messages could have easily been written out in advance, while the others had been scribbled out under duress, probably during the sitting. For these messages, it was possible that Slade had used a thimble with a piece of slate pencil attached to it, known among magicians as a "nail writer." Slade, it was thought, could easily have attached the thimble to an elastic up his sleeve and hurriedly copied out messages. The commission also speculated on other cheating techniques, including the use of disappearing chalk. Ultimately, it concluded that Slade's methods were "puerile in their simplicity."

Slade's fortunes declined. He continued to hold séances, but word spread of his chicanery and it seemed as if everyone was out to get him. The last noteworthy exposure happened in 1886 in Weston, West Virginia. While watching a séance from a crack under a door, two skeptics saw Slade move tables and chairs with his feet. Arrested and charged with fraud, Slade and his business manager were later released and the charges were dropped. The unfortunate episode was reported in the *Boston Herald* on February 2, 1886. Slade became an alcoholic and died, penniless, in a mental hospital in September 1905.

It's amazing that Slade was able to survive as long as he did, since very few internationally renowned mediums were caught cheating so often. His ascent and decline recalls Charles Foster, who also rose to great prominence, was exposed and died an impoverished alcoholic. In retrospect, slate writing seems as preposterous as other Spiritualist phenomena, but it speaks to the worldwide interest in charismatic mediums at the end of the 19th century. Since then, the polarization between skeptics and believers, which became evident in Slade's London trial, has grown immeasurably. To be sure, we still have mediums today, such as James Van Praagh and John Edward, but they are not subject to the same kind of public scrutiny from scientists.

James Van Praagh
TALKING TO HEAVEN

The credo of my life has always been: THE
UNKNOWN IS SOMETHING NOT YET FOUND.

—James Van Praagh

Why do people believe in ghosts? For many reasons, of course. Ghosts reassure us that death is not the end, that serious conflicts unresolved in life can be acted out in the afterlife or even solved. If, for instance, a man is killed by his wife and her lover, it seems fitting that his ghost would return to torment the adulterous couple; likewise, if a grandfather forges a special bond with his grandson but dies very suddenly, we might be willing to believe that his gentle spirit would haunt a place where they spent time together. The presence of ghosts can be comforting and can assuage our fear of death—even the fear we feel on behalf of others.

New Age medium James Van Praagh has made a healthy living off this feeling, although his approach had less to do with ghosts than with mediumship and self-empowerment. In the late 1990s, Van Praagh became a paranormal celebrity on the strength of a popular book about communicating with dead loved ones. He eventually parlayed his success into radio and television appearances and even a short-lived talk show. Yet in spite of his apparent novelty, Van Praagh was peddling the same snake oil as the Spiritualist mediums before him, proving that the need among the living to make contact with the dead is as powerful as ever.

Van Praagh was born around 1960 in Bayside, New York. His parents, observant Catholics, sent him to strict schools. When he was eight, a giant hand, pulsating with white light, appeared above his bed while he slept. It brought him a sense of peace and joy that he sought forever afterward. Taking this giant hand as a sign from God, Van Praagh became convinced that a world beyond the senses existed, although he kept it a secret.

At his mother's urging, Van Praagh left high school at 14 to study at Eymard Preparatory Seminary for aspiring priests. He realized that his views about God were more expansive and less rigid than the church's. After a year, he left and completed high school in the public system in New York City.

Van Praagh dreamed of becoming a famous Hollywood screenwriter. In 1978, he moved to the West Coast to major in broadcasting at San Francisco State University. But like many who go to California to pursue their dreams, he struggled to break through after his graduation. He got a job at the William Morris Agency with, in his words, "the glamorous responsibility of pulling staples out of files that were being prepared for microfiche."

One day, when he was 24, a coworker invited him to see the Spiritualist medium Brian Hurst. After the séance Hurst told Van Praagh that he would become a powerful medium. Though confused, he was also inspired to tune into his "emotional vibrations" through reading books and practice. Friends called him frequently to ask for advice, and Van Praagh showed remarkable insights into their personal lives. He eventually gave up a new job in the contracts department at Paramount Studios to give private readings, travel and conduct seminars. He founded a center in Los Angeles called Spiritual Horizons to coordinate his activities.

Van Praagh's first book, *Talking to Heaven: A Medium's Message on Life After Death*, appeared in 1997. Along with a brief narrative of his life, Van Praagh offers a crash course on physical and mental mediumship. Topics include condensed definitions of clairvoyance (seeing objects not in the visual field), clairaudience (hearing voices, often of the dead), spirit photography ("exact replications of deceased people on photographs") and apports (objects that materialize in a séance room), among others. He even affirms belief in "ectoplasm," a protean substance said to emerge from bodily orifices of mediums.

As evidence of his gifts, Van Praagh offers testimonials from his many readings with people who have contacted their dead loved ones with him acting as an intermediary. Almost every dramatic death scenario is covered, from suicides and car crashes to AIDS victims and euthanasia. In one case, Van Praagh relayed a message to a woman named Sydelle from her father, who had died after a battle with Alzheimer's. When she asked why the family had to endure the disease, the medium responded,

> He doesn't think you will understand it exactly, but believe it or not, he chose it before coming to earth. He is telling me he had to go through the experience to equal things out.

Van Praagh wraps up his book with some perspectives on death—how people can cope and how they can begin to contact the dead. To loosen up potential sensitives, he recommends a New Age staple—*chakras* or "centers of energy" scattered across the body—which can offer access to higher states of being when properly stimulated. He also recommends meditation and other spiritual exercises. Once prepared to communicate with the spirits, people can receive messages from them in many forms—through lights, clocks, telephones, even everyday appliances:

> Appliances have been known to stop or start working at different times when no one is around them. It is another way that spirits attempt to get our attention. I have found this quite common, especially if a spirit was very involved with cooking or spent much of its time in the kitchen area while alive.

As for motivation, Van Praagh claims that love should impel people to talk to heaven, and that they will be disappointed if they plan to pump the spirits for information on money, careers or relationships.

Talking to Heaven quickly became a best-seller and briefly reached number one on the *New York Times'* coveted list. Its runaway success inspired another book, *Reaching to Heaven: A Spiritual Journey Through Life and Death* (1999) and a number of lecture tours. The best evidence of Van Praagh's gifts came during lecture appearances and on several television shows and specials: *Living with the Dead*, a two-part miniseries on CBS, and the WB network's *Beyond with James Van Praagh*, an hour-long daytime talk show.

With a studio full of pre-screened audience members, Van Praagh would stage an impromptu group meditation before the cameras rolled. In a hypnotic voice he asked his sitters to close their eyes and focus on a positive image such as a blue sky or a rainbow. Then he instructed them to concentrate on their dead loved one, adding that he could "feel their pain." According to a reporter from Salon.com, who attended a séance of Van Praagh's in Arizona, many of the sitters began to cry at this point, perhaps sensing an emotional connection with the other side by way of the mesmerizing medium.

Van Praagh's technique, called "cold reading," is not new. It involves talking quickly, making safe guesses and carefully reading body language and verbal cues. He would often ask questions that seemed like statement of fact; in the split second that followed, he could gauge whether he was right and either follow up or switch to another question. The questions themselves concerned unresolved feelings, dead grandparents, marital difficulties, cancer and so on: overall, nothing risky for a crowd of entranced, largely middle-aged women. The goal was a meaningful narrative and, ultimately, cathartic contact with the dead.

According to observers, Van Praagh was wrong as often as he was right. One undercover observer noted that Van Praagh repeatedly prodded one woman about her belief in Jesus, only to discover that she was Jewish!

To his credit, Van Praagh never claimed to be infallible—nor, for that matter, to predict the future or to heal people—so his misses might seem inconsequential. As he makes clear in *Talking to Heaven*, his skills are at reading people, not being perfect:

> I don't want you to get the impression that
> I'm never wrong. Of course I am. I just want
> to explain that for me the easiest way to read

someone is through the emotions. The emotions are the rawest of energies, and whether
they realize it or not, most people wear their
hearts on their sleeves.

More to the point, Van Praagh's sitters are more prone
to overlook misses and focus on the hits. They attend or
watch his séances to *affirm* their belief in otherworldly
communication, *not* to question the entire enterprise.
They make an emotional, not necessarily rational, connection with the medium.

Inevitably skeptics were drawn to Van Praagh's very
public (and profitable) feats of mediumship. In a story in
the magazine *Skeptical Inquirer*, James Underdown and a
team of investigators attempted to determine whether Van
Praagh or the *Beyond* production team gathered information in advance from audience members or used other
means such as planted spies. Underdown noticed no hidden microphones or cameras for collecting data in advance,
nor did any of the fake names he provided turn up in Van
Praagh's readings. The most serious accusation he could
make involved the editing of *Beyond*. In several cases, it
appeared that what was taped for the show had been carefully edited, so some readings full of misses seemed more
favorable during broadcast. But such editing is common in
television production, since it helps to make awkward or
irrelevant stretches of live footage appear seamless.

Ultimately, Van Praagh did not appear to cheat as
some of his Spiritualist forbears had. Laura Laughlin, who
seemed skeptical before she attended a Van Praagh session, admitted on Salon.com afterward that:

I was sad and misty-eyed again after concentrating on my mom during the closing meditation. I was irritated by the sales pitches and the fact that all but one of the readings had involved someone in the expensive seats.

But I was also impressed. Van Praagh had made enough hits—and people's reactions had been so genuine—that I believed there was something to this, that he really might have special abilities.

What's more interesting than the comments of observers is the zealotry of Van Praagh's followers. A skeptic named Michael Shermer, who wrote up an exposure of Van Praagh in his book *Why People Believe Weird Things* (1997), got a frosty response when he sat in on a Van Praagh session and tried to alert the other sitters to his skeptical findings. According to Shermer, one woman "glared at me and told me it was 'inappropriate' to destroy these people's hopes during their time of grief."

Tribune Media Services cancelled *Beyond* in January 2003. The SciFi Channel, however, has kept a rival show, *Crossing Over with John Edward*, on its daytime rotation. Edward, whose background is not entirely unlike Van Praagh's, offers very similar results: contact with the dead through cold readings. It's possible that two medium-based shows were too many for the cable waves. Today, Van Praagh continues to publish books.

What explains Van Praagh's incredible success? His murky religious presentation was a major factor. During their heyday, Spiritualist mediums were associated with the occult, earning the scorn of organized religion. Van Praagh presented his new version of mediumship in an acceptably religious, not occult, context. He was a lapsed Catholic with a deep feeling for God, who argued that each of us is overseen by "guardian angels" or spirit guides. His angels were ethereal wispy beings, known more through imagery than any hard-line religious associations. They are sufficiently (although not totally) divorced from any particular sect of Christianity or any other faith. Perhaps the best evidence of Van Praagh's spirituality occurs in the acknowledgments of *Talking to Heaven* in which he thanks the " 'Creative Expression' identified under various titles such as God, Allah, Yahweh, Divine Being and the Great Light. I will just refer to this Power as the 'Source,' the Source of All."

If Van Praagh's loose spirituality struck a chord, his idea that "We are all born with some psychic ability" played an entire symphony. With this self-help theme, Van Praagh separated himself from earlier mediums, who set themselves apart from ordinary people through their unique paranormal abilities. Like fellow New Ager JZ Knight, he affirmed the God inside every person, claiming "each one of us is perfect if only we could seek our divinity," offering advice to people on how to hone their sensitivity and make contact with the dead.

Is death the end? Why do good people suffer and die needlessly? Can we make up for regrets in life by making contact with the dead? These are serious, timeless questions that Van Praagh raised and answered in his unique way.

6
Cult Figures

Aleister Crowley
SATAN'S DISCIPLE?

It's fitting that Aleister Crowley is a paranormal celebrity, since celebrities are often remembered superficially, through iconic images or scandals, and not for what they wanted to give to posterity. As his bizarre life makes clear, Crowley broke down barriers at every turn, changing the way we think about magic, mind-expanding drugs and open sexuality. But he was also a scoundrel and a listless wanderer, whose contributions to the paranormal are clouded by the desperate pleas for attention of a deeply unhappy man.

Crowley was born Edward Alexander Crowley in the English town of Leamington Spa in 1875. The son of a successful brewer, he was raised in strict accordance with the precepts of the Plymouth Brethren, a fundamentalist Christian sect for whom his father served as an elder. Crowley was initially devout, but soon wandered from the repressive code. Sensing this, his fanatical mother upbraided the recalcitrant youngster, especially after the death of his father when he was 11. Her habit of calling him the "the Beast," after the Antichrist in the Book of Revelation, would prove prescient. Crowley later described his mother as "a brainless bigot of the most narrow, illogical and inhuman type."

Crowley became interested in blood, torture and sexual degradation as a teen. Although he went to public schools, he managed to be accepted to Trinity College at

Cambridge University to study organic chemistry. Before dropping out, he cultivated his interest in the occult and honed his skills as a poet and mountaineer. A trust fund of £30,000, newly matured, allowed him the freedom he needed.

With the help of George Cecil Jones, an alchemist, Crowley was initiated into the London chapter of the Hermetic Order of the Golden Dawn (HOGD) in November 1898, at age 23. "Frater Perdurabo," as he called himself, began ascending to the 10th and highest "degree" of ceremonial magic—called "Ipissimus"—under the instruction of S.L. MacGregor Mathers, the head of the order. When Mathers had to leave for Paris, Crowley followed him but soon left to pursue theoretical training on his own. He went on to master yoga, tarot, Kabbalah and numerous other meditation traditions. One of his most cosmetic but lasting contributions was to spell "magic" as "magick"—in his words, "to distinguish the science of the Magi from all its counterfeits," i.e., stage magic.

Crowley's training in practical magick came by way of his friendship with fellow HOGD member Alan Bennett, a young engineer. The pair erected two magick temples in their Chancery Lane flat in London. Their White Temple, with an altar, mirror and other bizarre furniture, was used for traditional magick rituals. The more mysterious Black Temple also had an altar, but it was supported by a wooden sculpture of a black man standing on his hands as well as a skeleton. Crowley and Bennett sacrificed sparrows at this temple and used their blood to anoint it.

In 1899, after Crowley and a friend returned home after dining out, he noticed the altar overthrown in the

White Temple and the objects in disarray. Certain he had locked it before leaving, Crowley assumed the party responsible was not burglars but semi-materialized demons that he observed moving around the room. The young magician later had similarly eerie experiences at a mansion he purchased with some inheritance money near Loch Ness in Scotland.

In 1902 he met a highly unstable outsider called Rose Kelly; they soon married and headed to Cairo, Egypt, for their honeymoon. Although she had no previous interest in the occult, Kelly fell into a trance and received a spiritual message to contact the Egyptian god Horus, whose head was that of a hawk's. (Horus' eye, incidentally, remains a popular symbol of the occult.) Crowley entered into a trance in their room near the Cairo Museum and made contact with Horus' messenger, Aiwass. Over three days in April 1904, from noon to 1 PM, Kelly carefully transcribed the spirit communication, which was later published as Crowley's extended poem in prose, *The Book of the Law*. Heralding a new age of humanity, the book was intended to present a new liberal religion to unite all the world's conflicting faiths. It stands as Crowley's most famous publication.

The book shows many diverse influences, and its key theme has been as subject to as much misinterpretation as Nietzsche's announcement that "God is dead." Called the Law of Thelema, after the ancient Greek word for "will," it ran: "Do what thou will shall be the whole of the Law." This single directive, along with the directive, "Love is the law," was intended to replace Christianity's oppressive list of 10 stone commandments. Although many read

Crowley's law as a license for moral lawlessness, the message had more to do with self-fulfillment—one should do only what one must and nothing else.

Meanwhile, Crowley's marriage was showing some strain. Rose became pregnant and gave birth to a daughter named Lola Zaza. Following a pattern that defined many of his relationships, Crowley abandoned them both; Lola later died of typhoid during a trek in Vietnam. She was not the last of his children, legitimate or otherwise, to pass away. Rose became an alcoholic and eventually went mad.

Crowley was intent on spreading his newfound anti-gospel, convinced it would bring him fame. Adopting the title "the Great Beast of the Apocalypse," he founded his own order in 1907, Argentum Astrum (Latin for "Silver Star"), and began publishing a periodical called the *Equinox*. Alongside his own poetry, he revealed the ritual secrets of his former order, the Golden Dawn. His old mentor Mathers became so upset he tried unsuccessfully to get an injunction to stop Crowley, who thrived on this kind of negative publicity.

Meanwhile, Theodor Reuss, head of the German sex magick cult Ordo Templi Orientis (OTO), became fascinated with passages in *The Book of the Law* that hinted at the secret of his organization's Tantric sex rituals. He approached Crowley and convinced him to set up his own branch of the OTO.

To avoid military service in World War I, and to escape criticism for his pro-German stance, Crowley moved to the United States in 1914. He played a key role in OTO activities, helping to set up lodges in the United States and Canada. Crowley's time in the U.S. was generally uneventful and characterized by poverty and impatience. If anything, he is remembered for recruiting some bizarre disciples in the OTO lodges. One member in southern California, Jack Parsons, was a talented rocket scientist who fell deeply under the influence of "the Beast" and tried, as an homage, to write a fourth chapter of *The Book of the Law*. In the book *Sex and Rockets: the Occult World of Jack Parsons* (1999), John Carter tells Parsons' bizarre story, which involves L. Ron Hubbard (the best-selling creator of Dianetics) and Marjorie Cameron (the inspiration for the Eagles' song "Hotel California"), and ends under bizarre circumstances when Parsons blew himself up in his lab in 1952.

Crowley, meanwhile, managed to bring two mistresses home with him when he returned to England in 1919 following the Great War. Life was not a bed of roses, however. His asthma and bronchitis didn't agree with the damp British cold, and many of his friends had broken with him or settled down. When he unexpectedly received a legacy of £3000, he set off for warmer climes.

Crowley's lifestyle became increasingly excessive. His many mistresses were mostly lonely women and prostitutes from bathhouses, and his repeated attempts to conceive a "magickal child" were later chronicled in his novel *Moonchild* (1929). Not all of Crowley's partners were women—among his lovers was his former assistant, the poet Victor Neuberg, with whom he had an odd semi-sadistic fling.

Crowley also experimented with drugs such as opium and mescaline, which were thought to expand one's consciousness. Later in life he became addicted to heroin, and dictated several of his books while under its influence. His disciples quickly learned that drugs and Crowley were inseparable.

Crowley's excesses converged at a farmhouse in Cefalú, Sicily. As the setting for debaucherous orgies and rituals, his so-called "Abbey of Thelema" is probably most responsible for his reputation, given by a British newspaper, as "the wickedest man ever." Initially the Sicilians were willing to turn a blind eye to Crowley. But when Raoul Loveday, a brilliant Oxford graduate and Crowley disciple, visited with his wife Betty May, things got out of control. Within a day of a ritual involving the unsuccessful sacrifice of an animal, Loveday was dead, probably from a liver condition and possibly hepatitis. Appalled, his wife returned to England and crusaded against Crowley in the *Sunday Express* and other publications. "The Beast" was once again subject to the press' full venom. When Italy's new leader, Benito Mussolini, caught wind of the scandal, he ordered Crowley and his entourage to leave the country.

With his mistresses, disciples and children in tow, Crowley relocated to Tunis. But by this time he was hopelessly addicted to heroin. His excesses had drained his inheritances, while his books, mostly self-published and cast in a style inaccessible to the public, were not best-sellers during his life. He later left Tunis for Paris, then spent the rest of his days as a nomad, wandering through France and Germany, imposing himself on friends and others. As always, he found willing mistresses everywhere he went, but his life became increasingly pathetic and desperate.

In 1932 Crowley's old friend Nina Hammett, a sculptress, published a biography of him entitled *Laughing Torso*. Two years later, desperate for cash, Crowley sued her for libel, citing passages in which he is said to practice black magick and human sacrifice. After hearing the evidence, such as Crowley's pornographic poetry and twisted magickal rituals, the judge said that he had never heard such dreadful, blasphemous and abominable material as that produced by the man who described himself as the greatest living poet.

After this fitting tribute, the judge decided in Hammett's favor and dismissed all the charges. Crowley was finally bankrupt. By 1945, after years of listlessness, he moved into a humble boarding house in Hastings, England. There, at age 72, following a life in and out of the public eye, Crowley died in poverty. His cremated remains were sent to his followers in America. Along with many illegitimate children, he left behind a number of publications, fictional and non-fictional, some of which were published posthumously. None surpassed *The Book of the Law* as the most basic statement of his beliefs.

For all the controversy, Crowley led a relatively crime-free life. Besides the occasional animal sacrifice and the scandal surrounding the death of Loveday, he never committed a serious felony and his sexual affairs were unusual but consensual. His anti-Christian stance and his practice of magick clearly had intellectual, not anarchic, roots. If the British considered him evil, it was more for his Satanic beliefs than anything genuinely dangerous. Much of his desire was not to sin, but to earn fame by thumbing his nose at rigid English mores. Inevitably his repressive childhood was partly to blame. In his book *Occult America* (1972), John Godwin described Crowley as a "a grubby little boy thinly disguised as a monster."

Crowley's fame increased after his death, especially in popular music. He appears in the back row on the most famous album cover of all time, *Sgt Peppers Lonely Hearts Club Band* by the Beatles. In the early 1970s, "heavy metal" bands such as Black Sabbath became interested in Crowley, but more for his reputation as an iconoclast than anything he wrote or said. Jimmy Page, the celebrated lead guitarist of Led Zeppelin, bought Crowley's Scottish mansion and much of his memorabilia. It's perhaps ironic that Crowley died when he did, since his excessive lifestyle seems much better suited to rock and roll than to the relatively obscure world of magick.

Today, Crowley maintains an audience. In 1993 an album with his teachings was released and sold nearly 10,000 copies. *Megatherion*, the famous biography by Francis King, was reprinted in 2003 and attracted new interest. The same year, Crowley was named 73rd in the BBC's poll of the top 100 Britons. While his sycophantic followers exaggerate his influence by labeling him as a "misunderstood genius" or "the greatest magician of the 20th century," Crowley's status as a cult icon of the paranormal seems secure.

JZ Knight
RAMTHA'S CHANNEL

Ramtha. Glittering light and an unearthly presence, illu-
minating, pulsating, a vision perhaps of the grandiose
creative mind. The feeling of reality sweeping away the
objective consciousness of the real world. In what form
does one express the experience of an encounter with an
entity that modern-day life has yet to define?

—JZ Knight, *A State of Mind: My Story* (1987)

JZ Knight, an unlikely superstar of the New Age movement, became famous as a channel—someone contacted
by a spirit entity in much the same way that a medium
would rely on spirit controls. She was not the first. The
husband and wife team of Jane Roberts and Robert Butts
had put channeling on the culture map with their book
Seth Speaks (1972), in which an unseen entity communicated his wisdom to Jane while Robert wrote it down.
With "Ramtha," her incredibly ancient Cro-magnon
entity, Knight took channeling to a bizarre new level,
transforming his message of self-realization into a multimillion dollar empire.

JZ Knight was born Judith Darlene Hampton in 1946
in Roswell, New Mexico. Her parents were migrant farm
workers, and she was the eighth of nine children in a very
poor family. When Knight was five years old, her mother
left her alcoholic husband, Charles, and moved with her
children to Artesia, New Mexico.

After high school, JZ went to a business college but dropped out, choosing to focus on her marriage to Caris Hensley, an unfaithful, alcoholic gas jockey. They divorced in 1969 and Knight took a job as a cable TV saleswoman to support her two sons. At the time they lived in Roswell, New Mexico; her successful career took her to California and eventually Tacoma, Washington.

Her friends gave her the nickname "JZ." *J* was for "Judy" and *Z* for "zebra" since Knight loved to wear black and white clothing. Attractive and sunny with short blonde hair, she was a resourceful woman who never lacked male attention.

In the mid-1970s, she and a friend went to see a psychic who told her, rather cryptically, that she would move to a place with "great mountains" and "tall pines" and would meet "the One." By this time, Knight had met and married Jeremy Wilder, a dentist with occult leanings ("Jeremy Wilder" was a pseudonym given in Knight's autobiography). The couple shared a New Age fascination with pyramids, which were thought to harness spiritual energy.

One Sunday morning in July 1977, while she was examining a miniature pyramid in her kitchen, Knight had a vision. A powerful seven-foot tall man appeared before her, clad in a flowing robe and shimmering in a brilliant purple light. In Knight's words:

> He proclaimed, "I am Ramtha, the Enlightened One. I have come to help you over the ditch…It is the ditch of limitation." And he said, "I am here, and we are going to do grand work together."

Knight grew accustomed to being Ramtha's channel as she came to learn his remarkable story.

> Ramtha lived 35,000 years ago. He was born in Lemuria, a state in the ancient continent of Atlantis, in the middle of the Atlantic Ocean. It is a place undocumented in traditional history.

> This particular area of the world 35,000 years ago had a thriving spiritual civilization that went back even further to the time of dinosaurs, when very intelligent people lived or coexisted with reptilian beings.

When Ramtha was still young, misuse of advanced technology by the Atlatians led to a disaster that obliterated the northern part of the continent, including Lemuria. In the subsequent diaspora of Lemurians, Ramtha's family ended up in Onai, the great port city of Atlantis. There, Lemurians were subject to unfair treatment from their Atlatian overlords, who considered them soulless. This treatment angered the young Ramtha, who withdrew into the nearby mountains. Years later, with an army behind him, he returned to Onai and conquered the city. He was wounded, however, and needed time to recover.

During Ramtha's convalescence, he established contact with what he called the Unknown God. He realized that the warrior's thirst for blood was less important that the need to embrace life. To share this new wisdom with his people, Ramtha used the wind as a metaphor. Formless, limitless and free, it became the goal of Ramtha's spiritual exercises—to liberate himself from human limitations such as the body and even death. Eventually he had an out-of-body experience, which was followed by his transformation into light and his ascension to a higher plane. His promise to return, made originally to his own people, was fulfilled when he contacted JZ Knight.

By November 1978, Knight was ready to give her first public session. After initial successes, she began channeling Ramtha, also called "the Ram," during increasingly popular weekend gatherings called "dialogues." Clad in loose-fitting pants and an Indian tunic, she spoke in a strange accent, almost medieval or Elizabethan, and her voice became husky. Her posture and gait also changed and, according to some, even her eye color. These subtle shifts helped put followers more in touch with a figure from a radically different era. Ramtha, oddly enough, recommended that she charge money.

So why did Ramtha choose Knight as his instrument? The main reason, of course, was that Knight was unique and specially destined to relay his message. Another reason was that he wanted to discourage notions of his own superiority, since he affirmed the equality of all humans and their common inner divinity. Finally, conveying a kind of feminist message, he refused to be identified as a male religious figure; by channeling through a woman, he showed the equality that his message implied.

Ramtha's message wasn't original. According to J. Gordon Melton, an expert on religions and author of the sympathetic account *Finding Enlightenment: Ramtha's School of Ancient Wisdom* (1999), Ramtha's message is reminiscent of ancient Gnosticism. Each person is a master, even a god, who has lost contact with his or her origins. By coming to terms with one's own nature through increased consciousness (or Gnosis), an individual can take control of life and accomplish whatever one desires. This was "the Great Work" of which Ramtha spoke.

Ramtha's message of self-fulfillment was consistent with the burgeoning New Age movement, elements of which still appear in today's self-help literature. What made Ramtha noteworthy, at least as far as Knight presented him, was that he was a complex individual from the distant past, like Jesus Christ or Siddhartha. Yet he also proclaimed that a god dwelt in each person and insisted on the equality of all humans. With these ideas in mind, followers didn't mind that Ramtha's far-fetched existence on an imaginary continent was never proven—or even *could* be proven.

Knight traveled to Canada, Europe and Australia to spread Ramtha's teachings. The activity strained her marriage, and she soon left Wilder to be with Jeff Knight, whose picture she had seen in a magazine. Although Jeff had little interest in the occult, he became enthralled after attending a Ramtha dialogue at the home of actor Richard Chamberlain in 1980. Jeff was an accomplished equestrian rider and Arabian horse trainer, and he would figure in some of the scandals that beset his wife in the 1990s.

JZ Knight had gained a strong following by the early 1980s, but she still operated outside the mainstream. A brief endorsement from actress Shirley MacLaine, who paid for private sessions with Knight and described her own spiritual awakening in the breakthrough best-seller *Dancing in the Light* (1985), was a major windfall, as was support from Linda Evans of TV's *Dynasty*. With her popularity growing, Knight appeared on the *Merv Griffin Show* in 1985 and quickly emerged as the most famous of many figures in the world of channeling.

Then, in 1987, not long before the publication of her autobiography, *A State of Mind: My Story*, Knight established Ramtha's School of Enlightenment (RSE) on a sprawling 120-acre ranch in Yelm, Washington, south of Seattle. Her dialogues with Ramtha ceased, replaced by a structured course of Ramtha's teachings for the school's students.

Through meditation and unique breathing exercises, highly reminiscent of *pranayama* equivalents from India, Knight's students could overcome their limitations and tap into their divine natures, as Ramtha did. Some of the school's practices seemed to make sense only to insiders. One "field work" exercise involved leading students into a large field, blindfolding them and expecting them to find note cards attached to fence poles. Similar exercises took place in a maze called the Tank. According to Knight, all this training served to hone the "C&E" of the students—their "Consciousness and Energy." Most students were in their mid-30s, although some children have also participated.

As cult expert Joe Szimhart points out, Ramtha's message changed in the late 1980s and early 1990s, perhaps in keeping with growing anti-authoritarian paranoia. He predicted cataclysms and encouraged disciples to relocate to the Pacific Northwest for safe haven. At one point he warned, "When the dragon marches, be prepared to hibernate." Students were advised to stockpile supplies and build shelters that would protect them in the event of an attack from Chinese communist soldiers positioned in Mexico. It's unclear how Ramtha could know of these developments, or whether such paranoia is indicative of a cult.

Knight denies that the RSE is a cult. On her web site she maintains that:

> We are not a cult, although we do love the sacred...Ramtha's school is immersed in the sacred. And there has never been anyone in this school that has ever been harmed. We don't worship the devil. We don't worship anything negative. We are in love with the principle, and that principle is not Ramtha but ourselves.

RSE's students, it should be pointed out, are not brainwashed or bilked for money, and they are free to leave if they so desire. Some of the exercises described above, while odd, resemble activities used to initiate pledges into college fraternities. They are designed more to give participants a sense of accomplishment and comradeship than to coerce them into illegal behavior.

Regardless of the RSE's status, Ramtha became very lucrative, and some feel the school was heavily commercialized as Knight's success multiplied. There's no denying that she has parlayed an innocuous prophet into a multimillion dollar empire. Ramtha books and merchandise are available for sale on her web site, and Knight lives in a lavish French colonial mansion on her ranch.

To protect her valuable entity, Knight had Ramtha copyrighted, ensuring that she was the only one who could channel him or sell his message for money. Although various books and videotapes with Ramtha's teachings have emerged over the years, the most systematic and comprehensive presentation is still available only to students at the school.

Knight's exclusive control became important in 1997, when she discovered that a German woman named Judith Ravell, who had claimed to be Ramtha's true channel since 1992, was touring and conducting seminars. Knight immediately filed suit. The case reached the Austrian Supreme Court, and it decided in Knight's favor.

Knight's rise was accompanied by a number of public scandals. In the mid-1990s, she founded the Messiah Arabian Stud Ranch. Arabians were a popular breed at the time, and Knight claimed that Ramtha wished his followers to invest in the venture. Many students lost money and were disillusioned by the experience. To her credit, Knight eventually refunded the monies invested, although many people thought the damage had been done: she had used Ramtha's reputation for a goal entirely unrelated to his message.

A more damaging scandal emerged after Knight's marriage to Jeff Knight fell apart. Jeff, a bisexual, had contracted HIV sometime after 1987. By 1992 his health was in decline (JZ was never infected). He sued JZ in 1992, claiming that she had kept assets hidden from him and that he had been brainwashed to believe that Ramtha would restore his health. He felt he had been cheated out of a fair divorce settlement. Although the judge for the

Pierce County Superior Court dismissed charges of mind control, Jeff was awarded $750,000 based on the value of the estate when the couple married. This decision was overturned on appeal. Jeff died in 1994.

JZ Knight remains a key figure in the New Age movement. Following the mind-expanding "Age of Aquarius" in the 1960s, many sought solutions to complicated problems from sources unconnected to more traditional Western religions. Ramtha, a courageous warrior from "beyond the North Star" with the sensitivity of an Indian guru, seemed ideally suited to deliver an ancient message that incorporated contemporary notions about the women's movement, equality and the power of meditation. Regardless of Ramtha's doubtful origins, which critics are quick to point out, as well as claims that RSE is a cult, some of Knight's followers are faithful—or at least as much as can be expected from any New Age movement. Knight deserves credit for keeping their trust as "the Ram" became more about money than self-fulfillment.

Rasputin
SECRETS AND LIES

No figure connected with the paranormal seems to invite such wild inaccuracies as Rasputin. He has been called the "mad monk," even though he was neither a monk nor mad, and his duplicitous involvement with the Romanovs has led many, without much cause, to blame him for the end of the Russian monarchy and the rise of the Soviet Union. For years, many people even perpetrated the falsehood that his surname meant "licentious." The truth, like much of Rasputin's life, was much simpler: his name signified the intersection of two rivers, a fitting description of the small town where he was born and where the name is quite common.

Grigory Efimovich Rasputin was born in 1869 in Prokovskoe, a small village in Siberia on the banks of the Tura River. His parents were simple peasants, and their son quickly earned a reputation for troublemaking. He stole horses, drank to excess and liked to dance to gypsy music. As he matured, his sexual appetite became ravenous; with exceptions here and there, his libido would remain unbridled to his dying day.

Rasputin's first glimmerings of religious feeling came around age 16, when he joined the Verkhoturnye Monastery. He found a new spiritual conviction during three months with hermits and wise elders, although it should be noted that he was no less inclined to indulge his vices after leaving.

Contrary to popular opinion, Rasputin was not a member of the Khlysty, a dissenting sect of the Russian Orthodox Church. This sect, which dismissed priests, books and saints and caused tremors in Russian society, claimed that the path to grace lay in ritualized sexual indulgence, which often took the form of large orgies and flagellation. Rasputin never joined, even if the idea that sin is a necessary part of redemption was not only a justification for his lifestyle, but also an essential part of his seduction technique.

Rasputin made several pilgrimages to holy sites, including the Holy Land, ingratiating himself in high society and among religious authorities along the way. In turn, they offered him introductions in St. Petersburg, then the name for Petrograd. He arrived in the city in 1903, in his mid-30s. The well-traveled *starets* (religious pilgrim) made an immediate impact among church leaders with his stories and mysterious gifts, which included healing. Russia at the time was an oppressive regime ruled by an elite monarchy, so Rasputin benefited from the popularity of Spiritualism. Members of the ruling classes were prone to believe in occultists and faith healers—or at least have them in their drawing rooms and gab about it for days afterwards.

Rasputin's appearance was a part of his mystique. Tall and mysterious looking, he wore either a monk's robe or a peasant tunic and large boots. His hair and beard were long and greasy, and he was famous for never washing. His outstanding feature, however, was his gaze. Of his pupils, one observer said "they sparkled with phosphorescent light. He sort of groped listeners with his eyes." The effect was pronounced on women. Among those whom he entranced were two grand duchesses, Militsa and Anastasia, called "the crows" for their dark hair and chattering ways; they would later play a key role in Rasputin's rise. But for the time being, the Siberian peasant was content to indulge in his growing list of vices and to make powerful contacts.

At the end of the 19th century, the Russian monarchy was in an awkward spot. Tsar Alexander III, a powerful man with extensive military training, had died unexpectedly in 1894 at age 49. His son Nicholas had been coddled by his mother, the Empress Maria Feodorovna, and lacked the political sophistication to oversee the vast Russian empire. Nevertheless, he became tsar at 26 and was expected to ruthlessly suppress agitators at home while tending to increasing threats from abroad.

Nicholas' affection for Princess Alix of Hesse further complicated matters. He and the melancholy princess were third cousins, and she was a cherished granddaughter of Queen Victoria. But Alix was from Germany, and as such was unacceptable to the Romanovs and to other powerful parties in Russia.

The couple's wedding was expedited on account of the tsar's ill health—for Nicholas to be unmarried and heirless upon becoming tsar would have been a serious concern. The pair were married in the Russian Orthodox Church not long after Alexander's death, and Alix took the name Empress Alexandra Feodorovna, the Tsarina.

The royal couple was highly devoted to each other, happy to live in seclusion at Alexander Palace in Tsarskoe Selo, a healthy distance from the gossip-ridden circles of

Russian society. Alexandra's responsibility was to produce an heir, but, to her great consternation, she gave birth to four daughters in the first decade of marriage. The Romanovs prayed desperately for a male child.

The birth of Alexis in 1904 was a mixed blessing. The couple finally had an heir, but when the young tsarevich was injured and bled without any sign of clotting, his mother feared the worst. The diagnosis—hemophilia—was not altogether unexpected: a handful of Queen Victoria's descendants suffered from the hereditary blood condition, which could become fatal if untreated. Some, including Queen Victoria's youngest son Prince Leopold, had even died of it.

Given his royal destiny, Alexis' parents worried constantly about his health. Armies of doctors claimed that further episodes were inevitable and would probably kill the boy. Blaming herself, the supernaturally inclined tsarina dismissed their speculations, confident that prayer or other means could cure the boy. By consulting all manner of religious figures and mystics, the stage was set for the appearance of a miracle worker.

Meanwhile, in an attempt to extend their own influence, Militsa and Anastasia recommended Rasputin, who had returned after a two-year absence. According to some sources, the introduction that followed became a decisive moment in the history of the Russian monarchy.

The first healing episode, perhaps not entirely credible, took place sometime in 1907. Rasputin was summoned after the boy bruised himself and developed a fever. Rasputin arrived at the boy's bedside and prayed fervently for his recovery. After a short spell, the boy was happily asleep, breathing normally. The Romanovs were amazed.

In keeping with his peasant upbringing, Rasputin was unusually familiar around the royal family. Nicholas called him "our friend" and Alexandra immediately took to him. Meanwhile, Rasputin continued with his drinking and womanizing, but now also boasted of his growing pull with the royal family. When the tsar's secret police got wind of Rasputin's boasting, Nicholas was furious and summoned Rasputin. Although Alexandra pleaded his case, the *starets* was sent away to the provinces as punishment.

But Rasputin's way with Alexis assured his return and privileged position. In 1912 the boy slipped and badly bruised himself while getting out of a boat. While most children recovery quickly from such a spill, it could extremely painful to a hemophiliac, since the bruise could continue to bleed under the skin and affect nearby joints and muscles. When Alexis' fever rose, doctors worried for his life. Alexandra's closest confidant, Anna Vyrubov, urged her to contact Rasputin, who was thousands of miles away in Prokovskoe. He telegraphed back, "The illness is not as dangerous as it seems. Don't let the doctors worry him." Miraculously, the boy's condition improved soon after this missive was sent.

Another healing happened after Alexis accidentally struck the window of a train, causing his nose to bleed. Rasputin was again consulted, but he delayed for a full day before responding. By the time he arrived, the boy's condition was serious. Again, the healer's mysterious presence seemed to stop the bleeding.

*Rasputin, surrounded by members of the Romanov circle, had a
mesmerizing effect on women.*

Rasputin's healing gifts have never been sufficiently explained. Some people argue he used hypnosis on the tsarevich, although it's unlikely he would have ever learned such a technique and it fails to explain how he could have healed Alexis remotely. Others believe that the boy suffered not from hemophilia but aplastic anemia, a condition that carries similar symptoms but is marked by unexplainable bouts of spontaneous remission. Either way, Rasputin's healing touch ensured his continued presence at the royal residence, and allowed him to ply his influence with the Romanovs.

By this point, many influential parties sought Rasputin's head. Since the royal family had kept Alexis' hemophilia from their subjects and had tried to keep Rasputin's presence at their home a secret, many were unaware of his healing gifts. Those who knew of his visits often speculated wildly on his motives, based on rumors or Rasputin's drunken bragging about his sway with the royals.

As evidence of his excessive lifestyle emerged, religious authorities who once supported Rasputin came to see him as an agent of the Devil and an apostate. Aristocrats lumped him in with the German-born tsarina, who was fittingly called "the foreigner"; she returned their spite in kind. People were outraged that Rasputin helped secure the dismissal of established ministers in favor of his questionable, even corrupt, favorites. It was simply too much from a Siberian peasant.

The first attempt on his life took place in spring 1914. It was around the time that Archduke Franz Ferdinand was killed in Sarajevo, setting off the chain of events that led to World War I. At the behest of a monk named

Iliodor, an envious rival of Rasputin's, a misshapen prostitute named Khioniya Guseva stabbed Rasputin in the abdomen while he was in Prokovskoe. She then declared, quite prematurely, "I've killed the Antichrist!" Although seriously wounded but not dead, Rasputin reached down for a piece of wood and hit her over the head while angry villagers grabbed and threatened her. He was critically ill for 10 days, but under the care of doctors Rasputin recovered. His resilience, as a subsequent assassination attempt would show, was almost superhuman.

When war broke out in 1914, the suspicion of the Romanovs grew. Under Nicholas' inept leadership, Russia was ill equipped to go to war against the Germans and Austrians. The military was corrupt, supply lines were inadequate and Nicholas was not trained to handle the mounting crisis. When he dismissed his cousin, Grand Duke Nicholas Nicholayevitch, as head of the military in 1915, perhaps under Rasputin's influence, he made a fatal miscalculation. Taking up the post himself, the tsar was forced to move to military headquarters, in effect leaving Empress Alexandra to oversee matters in his absence—with Rasputin lurking behind the scenes.

The tsar's family and his mother pleaded with Nicholas to remove Rasputin from the home. Nicholas, reluctant to displease his wife or place his son's health in jeopardy, refused their pleas. In Russian social circles a refrain was often heard: "Something has to happen."

Rasputin was murdered on December 29, 1916. Shortly before, he felt a strange forboding. In a letter he showed to Alexandra he made a chilling prediction. If the peasants killed him, he wrote, the monarchy would prosper; if the nobility slew him, the Romanovs would perish within two years and the aristocracy would be plagued with troubles for 25 years.

The ringleader was Prince Felix Yusupov, a thin, attractive man who was a closet homosexual. He was married to the tsar's beautiful niece Irina, and stood to inherit a family fortune, so his motives seemed unclear. His co-conspirators were Grand Duke Dmitry Pavlovich, a cousin of the tsar, and Vladimir Purichkevich, a prominent politician who had recently made a rabidly anti-Rasputin, anti-Alexandra speech on the floor of the Duma, Russia's lower parliament. Several others, including a doctor named Lazavert, were also involved but played less direct roles in the murder.

Yusupov, who had surreptitiously befriended Rasputin, lured him to see Irina, with the tacit promise of a sexual encounter. In fact, Irina was far away in the Crimea. Picking up Rasputin shortly after midnight, although not entirely in secret as Yusupov had planned, the prince brought him to his family palace on the Moika Canal in St. Petersburg. Yusupov had prepared a basement room to make his victim feel particularly at home. Separated into a dining and living room, it was an inviting space, with a bright fire blazing in the hearth and a polar bear skin rug. A door led to a courtyard outside.

The assassins had laid out their scheme earlier that night. To avoid making a ruckus, they decided to poison Rasputin instead of shooting him. Doctor Lazavert added lethal doses of potassium cyanide to some pastries and wine, leaving some unpoisoned for Yusupov. Perhaps showing his lack of foresight, the doctor tossed his rubber gloves in the fireplace, filling the room with smoke and stench. Other blunders followed as the plot unfolded. Though the perpetrators had planned out the crime to the last detail, the murder became an unpredictable marathon.

The pair arrived and Yusupov led his guest downstairs. Noise echoed upstairs, including the song "Yankee Doodle Dandy," and the prince blamed unexpected company, which Irina was required to entertain; he promised she would be down shortly. Taking his cue, Yusupov offered up the laced delicacies. At first Rasputin refused to eat them; he also declined the wine since he preferred Madeira. Yusupov pressed, and the *starets* ate the pastries and drank the wine. The prince settled in, awaiting the inevitable. It never came. Desperate, he adjourned to check on the visitors upstairs.

Upon his return, Rasputin asked him to play some gypsy music on a guitar in the room. As time dragged on, Yusupov was required to make new excuses for Irina's absence. By 2:30 AM, the poison, whose effects were supposed to be instantaneous, had not worked. Rasputin seemed tired, but after downing another glass of wine he instantly revived.

Again, Yusupov went upstairs, this time returning with a heavy revolver given to him by Purichkevich. Noticing his victim playing with the drawers in an ivory cabinet, he approached Rasputin and said, "Grigory Efimovich, you would do better to look at the Crucifix and pray to it." Then he shot him in the heart.

The others rushed downstairs. To prevent blood from soaking into the rug, they moved the victim. Then they noticed that he was still breathing. After waiting a few minutes, Rasputin convulsed violently then became silent. Assured he was finally dead, the relieved conspirators decided to take a break at around 3 AM. The next step involved having one of them dress up in Rasputin's cloak and hat and be driven home by the others, giving any secret police the idea he was still alive. Then Pavlovich and Lazavert would return to the palace, drag the body away and dump it in the river through a hole in the ice.

After a while Yusupov was possessed by a desire to look at the body again; why exactly, no one knows. When he began to shake the corpse, Rasputin suddenly awoke and grabbed Yusupov's shoulders. According to the prince, his eyes bulged from their sockets and his grip was like iron. Yusupov managed to free himself and dash upstairs, but not before Rasputin had ripped an epaulet from his military uniform.

While Yusupov frantically explained what had happened, Rasputin stumbled up the stairs and headed for an iron gate that opened on to the street. Purichkevich gave chase, listening to Rasputin rail against his assassin, declaring he would tell all to the empress. He aimed his pistol and shot. Although he was an accomplished shooter, he missed; he fired a second time, again missing his mark. Finally, after biting his hand to steady it, he aimed and struck Rasputin in the shoulder. A fourth bullet appeared to enter his head. The fallen man attempted to crawl with his final strength. Purichkevich ran to the body and kicked it as hard as he could; Yusupov soon joined him and brutalized the body and face with a club. Both assumed it was finally over.

Meanwhile, a policeman named Vlassiyev had heard the shots. He came to investigate and was told by Purichkevich, incredibly, that Rasputin had been "dispatched." Soon after, sensing his mistake, the influential Purichkevich swore the officer to silence. The body, wrapped in a curtain or a carpet, was loaded into his car and driven north of the city. The conspirators tossed it into the Neva River, struggling at first to get it over the railing. Exhausted and confused, they had forgotten to weigh the body down. A telltale boot lay on the ice.

The police investigation quickly revealed the guilty parties, especially after the officer at the scene reported to his superiors. But the men involved were not tried or arrested, in spite of indignant pleas from Alexandra. The entire nation had turned on her and Rasputin, and some of the murderers were related by blood to Nicholas. To avoid any implication of Romanov involvement, Purichkevich and Yusupov explained that the other conspirators were not present at his house. Yusupov's explanation of the night's events was ridiculous. He said he had held a party with many women and someone had shot a dog early in the morning as a joke, which explained the blood and noise. This explanation was utter nonsense. Later, having been exiled, Yusupov wrote an account of the murder, on which others are loosely based.

The body turned up on December 19, near the bloodied boot. The autopsy showed the bullet wounds and the contusions were consistent with the account given above; however, the medical examiner found alcohol but no poison. Some argue the inefficacy of the poison was attributable to Rasputin's chronic gastritis, which delayed its absorption. It's also possible that no poison was actually used. Yusupov may have invented the detail to add credibility to Rasputin's supernatural reputation, which was amplified by the additional details of his unkillability. Whatever the case, a small notice appeared in the paper announcing Rasputin's death.

The end of the Romanov dynasty was at hand. Within three months, revolutionaries ousted the family; the following year, the entire royal family was shot to death.

Rasputin's role in the end of the Russian monarchy is often exaggerated. Given the complexity of the mounting crisis, it's no surprise that some people singled him out as a scapegoat. Following his death, his reputation grew, for better or for worse. Among the communists, he was dismissed as a symbol of the old world order that perished with the monarchy; the peasants, on the other hand, saw him as a much-maligned man of the people and folk hero. Even today, in spite of new information about his sexual escapades, perhaps even with Alexandra, some religious groups argue for his martyrdom.

Sybil Leek

FAMOUS WITCH

One of the mainstays of the anti-witch craze was the so-called witches' *sabbat*, a demonical orgy in which witches were said to gorge themselves on vile foods, dance around a blazing fire and boast of their evil works. As they lost themselves in the ecstatic proceedings, a seething cauldron might have bubbled over with a noxious brew made from the crushed-up bones of infants, obtained either from the local graveyard or through murder. Some demonologists even believed that witches flew on broomsticks to these gatherings, generally on the outskirts of town, and that one of the highlights of the night involved lining up behind Satan, who was always the guest of honor, and kissing his posterior. This was called the *osculum infame* or Kiss of Shame.

Satan, of course, was not content merely to have his butt kissed. To conclude the Bacchanalian *sabbat*, new witches were expected to mate with him, with hopes of conceiving a devil child. The next morning, probably hungover from the mead and the revelry, witches could presumably get back to their day-to-day activities of mixing potions, spoiling crops and cursing livestock with disease.

In retrospect, the witches' *sabbat* seems fantastic, even laughable. It hinted vaguely at the origins of witchcraft in fertility cults and prehistoric systems of belief, but it blew everything wildly out of proportion, especially with the ideas that witches practice magic and were in league with the Devil, which were simply never the case.

Even though you might expect us to know better in the 21st century, many of the prejudices and misconceptions surrounding witchcraft persist today. While no one honestly believes witches wear pointed hats or have warts and pointy noses, contemporary Wiccans are not well understood or unduly ignored. Their desire to give witchcraft credibility is not new, however. After World War II, a prominent British witch named Sybil Leek crusaded to show modern witchcraft in an entirely new light and in so doing became something of a celebrity herself.

Leek was born in 1917 in Staffordshire, England. Her family was relatively well off, and Leek later claimed that her ancestors on both sides had occult connections. Her father was close to mystics at the court of the Russian tsars, while her mother's ancestors had practiced the "Old Religion" in southern Ireland in the 12th century. Leek's most famous ancestor was a witch called Molly Leigh, who died in 1663. Apparently after Leigh died, her ghost appeared at her cottage with a jackdaw perched on its shoulder. The local religious authorities, suspecting the work of the Devil, had the body exhumed, plunged a stake into its heart and then threw a dead jackdaw into the coffin.

Leek's grandmother taught her at home until she was 12; she finished her education at local schools. While she never earned a college degree, her inclination for writing allowed her to write many books later in life. When Leek was 15, she met a pianist and conductor who was 24 years her senior. They married about a year later and traveled extensively across Europe. When he died suddenly, the 18-year-old Leek returned home to Hampshire.

During World War II, the young witch worked as a nurse for the Red Cross in a military hospital near Southampton. She moved around in this capacity, treating the wounded in various places in England and Scotland. After the war, she settled in Burley, a small village close to New Forest.

One of the oldest forests in England, New Forest was a kind of epicenter of modern British witchcraft. In 1939, Gerald Gardner, a retired civil servant who had lived much of his life in the Far East, was initiated into a coven of New Forest witches by "Old Dorothy" Clutterbuck. Gardner kept the activities of his coven secret, but he became a respected spokesman for a modern pagan movement, spearheading a revival of the Old Religion with his books *Witchcraft Today* (1954) and *The Meaning of Witchcraft* (1959).

Leek joined the Horsa Coven, a longstanding but secret group. She was said to have been anointed as the high priestess of the 700-year-old group. Leek's kinship with the local gypsies was also remarkable, since they were notoriously suspicious of outsiders. Not only did she learn about potions from them, they also made her a "blood sister," which involved cutting her wrist and mixing the blood with that of fellow gypsies.

To make ends meet, Leek ran an antique store in Burley. The media took notice of her activities in witchcraft and astrology; the Witchcraft Act was still on the books until 1951 and the British were suspicious of anything pagan. People flocked to the store to get the witch's autograph. Unhappy with the attention, Leek's landlord refused to renew her store's lease unless she desisted from her activities in the Old Religion. Leek refused and was forced to close up shop. She was ready to begin a new chapter in her life.

Leek accepted an invitation to the United States in the early 1960s; at the time, modern witchcraft was virtually unknown there. In 1964 she moved to New York with her second husband Brian and their two sons. Soon they headed off for Los Angeles, where Leek said she met Aleister Crowley's secretary Israel Regardie.

Later Leek opened a restaurant, called Sybil Leek's Cauldron, in Houston, which became her base of operations. She split her time between Texas and Florida, overseeing covens in Massachusetts, Cincinnati and St. Louis; she was also an accomplished astrologer who played an important role in popularizing horoscopes.

Leek's appearance, for better or for worse, matched her reputation. A robust woman with aquiline nose and bushy eyebrows, she fit the image of a witch and fortune-teller, clad in loose gowns and capes with Hotfoot Jackson, her pet jackdaw bird, perched on her shoulder. Leek kept two boa constrictors and always wore crystal necklace passed on to her by her psychic Russian grandmother.

Her fame grew on the basis of her media appearances in America and around the world, organized with the help of public relations staff. Although she was a tireless self-promoter who never turned down an opportunity to make money or multiply her renown, Leek helped to fight popular stereotypes, still in place today, of witches as hags.

She also covered a battery of arcane subjects in the 60 or so books she wrote; the topics included astrology, ghost hunting, séances and other paranormal phenomena. Her most famous are *Diary of a Witch* (1968), which explored her struggle for legitimacy as a witch, and *The Complete Art of Witchcraft* (1971), considered something of a classic in the field.

Leek presented the Old Religion in a bold new light. Guided by the spirit of Madame Helena Blavatsky, cofounder of the Theosophical Society, she emphasized the ancient principles of life such as reincarnation and argued against the popular identification of witchcraft with Satanism. In an interview reported in John Godwin's *Occult America* (1971), Leek said witchcraft

> is not anti-Christian and not heathen. It's the Old Religion because it seems to go back to the time when man was first on earth, and when he had those religious, spiritual feelings. I think it's a great mistake to think that man did not have religion until Christ and Buddha appeared.

She was also one of the first witches to discuss the environmental side of Wicca. Her beliefs, it should be noted, were often not in keeping with other traditions in witchcraft. By opposing the use of nudity and drugs in rituals, Leek marched to her own drummer.

After a long battle with cancer, Sybil Leek died on October 28, 1982, in Melbourne, Florida. She was only 65.

Her obituary in the *New York Post* was entitled "Requiem for a Witch."

Sybil Leek sought celebrity through witchcraft. A critical look at her autobiography reveals what appear to be many invented episodes. Leek, for instance, wrote in her autobiography that she had known Aleister Crowley since she was nine, when he was a regular visitor at the family home. She explained that they went hiking together, and he played a key role in her development as a witch.

Very little of this has any basis in fact. When run against a time line of Aleister Crowley's life, Leek's meeting with him appears to have been manufactured. Her claim to have met Israel Regardie in America seems equally unfounded. Leek simply used Crowley's name to associate herself with a celebrity and in doing so become one herself. Ironically, this craving for public acclaim was also a trait of Crowley's, although it ran counter to Leek's ultimate goal: to bring a new respectability to modern witchcraft. Fortunately, her deception appears to have gone undiscovered during her life, although it may be a factor among contemporary Wiccans, who continue the struggle to overturn witch stereotypes today.

The End